GRILL
FIRE

GRILL
FIRE

100+ RECIPES & TECHNIQUES
FOR MASTERING THE FLAME

LEX TAYLOR

STERLING EPICURE
New York

STERLING EPICURE
New York

An Imprint of Sterling Publishing Co., Inc.
1166 Avenue of the Americas
New York, NY 10036

Text © 2017 by Lex Taylor
Photographs © 2017 by Sterling Publishing Co., Inc., except as noted in the photo credits on page 206

ISBN 978-1-4549-2151-6

Library of Congress Cataloging-in-Publication Data

Names: Taylor, Lex, author.
Title: Grill fire / Lex Taylor.
Description: New York, NY : Sterling Publishing Co., Inc., [2017] | Includes
 index.
Identifiers: LCCN 2016044026 | ISBN 9781454921516
Subjects: LCSH: Barbecuing. | Outdoor cooking. | LCGFT: Cookbooks.
Classification: LCC TX840.B3 .T334 2017 | DDC 641.7/6--dc23 LC record available
at https://lccn.loc.gov/2016044026

Distributed in Canada by Sterling Publishing Co., Inc.
c/o Canadian Manda Group, 664 Annette Street
Toronto, Ontario, Canada M6S 2C8
Distributed in the United Kingdom by GMC Distribution Services
Castle Place, 166 High Street, Lewes, East Sussex, England BN7 1XU
Distributed in Australia by NewSouth Books
45 Beach Street, Coogee, NSW 2034, Australia

For information about custom editions, special sales, and premium and corporate purchases, please contact
Sterling Special Sales at 800-805-5489 or specialsales@sterlingpublishing.com.

Manufactured in China

2 4 6 8 10 9 7 5 3 1

www.sterlingpublishing.com

Design and layout by Gavin Motnyk
Food styling by Justin Nillson + Jo Obarowski
Photography by Bill Milne + Chris Bain + Lex Taylor
For photo credits, see page 206

CONTENTS

INTRODUCTION

I am by varying accounts a normal hominid. I stand upright, I have a haircut, I speak in civilized tones, and I use familiar hand gestures. I even know some jokes (all shameful and disgusting). When I'm in public, I wear pants and usually refrain from doing dastardly things. I even own a small software company, write code, and design flashy things. Days are spent working in tandem with other civilized hominids, going to meetings, taking minutes, notes, and recording follow-ups. I work well with others, and once in a while I impress everyone at work with a very clever email.

But often, as has been the case since I was very young, my mind wanders—not to some dystopian future, but to the distant past. In these wanderings there are landscapes of vast and icy mountains, Cretaceous jungles, and biblical storms. I imagine the first protohumans—prey!—standing at the edge of a huge coniferous forest, hungry, cold, and afraid. During these times fire was our only friend. With it we warmed our spirits, fended off wild beasts, and then ultimately cooked those creatures!

O, to exist back in the all-or-nothing days, before the Undo button, when everything mattered, when we lived with nature and survived—if we actually did—on horse sense and sheer intuition!

To be bored was a good thing. It meant that you weren't being chased down by a saber-toothed tiger, your dinner plans were secure, and the kids weren't sinking into quicksand. You had time on your hands. And you used those hands, the greatest tools ever, to build shelter, fashion tools, and hunt for survival, not peck away at an iPhone. I imagine what it would have been like to look up at the stars, not knowing in the slightest what they were. And, with our puzzled imaginations, to make up stories about them and then tell those stories around the fire. My doctor diagnosed me with attention deficit hyperactivity disorder (ADHD) and dosed me hard with Ritalin, but I think the reality is that I was just born in the wrong century.

As a dreamer, art has always been my way of knowing. It speaks to all those things that have no language for self-expression. Art allows us to explore the multiverse of our imagination. And like the paintings of Caravaggio or the concertos of Brahms, food too speaks to the soul and its cavernous depths. To eat is to consume culture, acknowledge history, and celebrate life. And whether we're tenderly dining on tapas, overlooking the Alhambra at dusk, or drunkenly gorging ourselves at a Brooklyn White Castle at 4 a.m., food enlightens and satisfies.

As an artist I make leather bags, knives, grills, tables, and chairs. I'm an illustrator, photographer, designer, and chef. I have mastered the hardest culinary challenge, the smoked brisket, multiple times. But understanding my phone bill? Putting together my Tupperware so the lids fit? Filling out an immigration form correctly the first time, or even the fourth? Impossible. In many modern scenarios I struggle with the most basic tasks like a befuddled infant.

I am drawn to grilling because to grill *is* to be human in a timeless continuum. Cooking meat over fire can be traced back to when ancient protohumans first grabbed a fistful of smoldering beast from a bushfire and thought, "What could possibly go wrong?" Cave-dweller cookouts were the seminal invention that contributed to the rise of modern humans. Cooking food allows our intestines to absorb about 75 percent more of the available calories, and over a half million years later, our enlarged brains have encouraged us to invent the baconator, the spiralizor, the Clapper! Historically speaking, we are far more adept at grilling meats and making fire than anything else, other than sex. Grilling is in our blood; it's instinctual. As we have become more "civilized," much of our intuition and "horse sense" has been replaced with gadgets and gizmos that promise convenience, while slowly whittling us down to dull stumps—domesticated, housebroken, pusillanimous primates.

I have had the great fortune to travel my whole life, from the Rockies to the Andes to the Swiss Alps; from the jungles of West Africa to the fjords of the Arctic; and from the Mojave to the Sahara and the Atacama Desert—always with an eye on new foods and techniques, and with the mission to acknowledge and celebrate that astonishing diversity back at home. How can great spices, herbs, and cooking techniques from around the world be applied to my backyard barbecues? How can I keep dishes I devise new and exciting while still keeping them familiar and fun?

Part of the joy of grilling is that it is ritualistic and familiar, but I know from experience how much my guests love to be wowed and experience different takes on the classics. In this book I want to share many of the wonderful grilling techniques I've learned and the flavors I have experienced in my travels, while keeping, for the most part, a steady eye on American staples, whether it's a simple hamburger or an exquisitely but simply grilled steak.

I have nothing against gas grills, digital thermometers, and purple, heatproof meat-handling gloves that can be snagged for 50 percent off their original 200 percent markup. These tools are easy, and anything that makes it easy to be outside, comfortably cooking and spending time with family, is a good thing. But the idea I want to get across in this book is that these tools are totally unnecessary and distract from the elemental *art* of grilling, the understanding of wood, the appreciation of steel, the making and managing of fire and food. It's all about creating flavors and experiences that cannot be duplicated in the kitchen or bought online! At its core, grilling is about love and respect for the first art.

As a world traveler, I am constantly trying new foods, new flavors, and new cooking techniques. I eat everything and will try anything, from raw seal and fermented walrus to camel-milk cappuccinos. I enjoy a 19-course tasting menu at Santiago, Chile's Boragó restaurant or simply eating bugs. I love discovering new combinations, textures, colors, and ways of playing with temperatures. The more I discover, the more I realize how much room there is to be creative with food and how much people respond to new, exciting, grilled dishes. I hope this book awakens the same spirit of excitement and creativity and inspires you to try something new the next time you fire up the grill.

MEAT & FIRE: GRILLING BASICS

What any grill master aims for is a perfect, caramelized outer crust, or bark, and a perfectly pink center. To achieve this consistently with different thicknesses of meat directly over a finicky fire is the ultimate goal. In its most simple sense, thinner cuts cook at a higher temperature with less time, and thicker cuts cook at a lower temperature for more time. We want the inside to get to the perfect temperature exactly when the outside forms the perfect bark. The matter gets complicated when coals change temperature, flare-ups occur, and meats with different thicknesses, such as chicken breasts, are cooked. However, direct grilling only applies to certain cuts of meat. Cuts from the upper legs, neck, and chest, such as top round, blade, and brisket, respectively, are tough, fibrous muscles that can be utterly divine but are not necessarily right for fast direct grilling; they are commonly used in low and slow smokers. One way around this is to slice these cuts thin, marinate them, and then sear them; however, telling pit masters that instead of smoking a brisket for 20 hours you prefer to cut it thin and sear it won't necessarily make you friends.

DIRECT GRILLING

The setup for direct grilling will depend slightly on the shape and size of the grill and exactly what you plan to cook. Round Weber Original Kettle™ and Big Green Egg® grills are deep and efficient due to their convecting shapes, as contrasted with barrel grillers/smokers, which tend to have a lot of grill surface area over a long, shallow trough. But 90 percent of these grills all cook a great four-person meal with a single chimney's worth of coal or wood. Gas grills too have great surface area and can achieve a very organized temperature spectrum, if the controls are used as instructed by the manufacturer's manual.

Here are some pointers for building a fire and grilling direct:

1 | For briquettes or lump coal, fill the top part of a chimney to the brim and add a few pages of balled-up newspaper to the bottom; then ignite the newspaper. I'll usually do this right in my grill. Note that the beginning of this process will create a lot of heavy smoke, so be sure to light away from the house or far from outside drying laundry. Briquettes will take about 20 minutes to get piping hot; lump coal, depending on the size of the chunks, will take 10 to 15 minutes. You will know the coals are ready for cooking when steady flames are seen coming from the top of the chimney. You will also know in a matter of minutes if you accidentally used match-light coal, as your chimney will turn into a giant blowtorch and possibly ignite all your drying clothes. Please avoid this. Also note that lump coal will spit embers once it gets going (and a lot of embers will appear when your pour them out into the grill). I have never injured myself with these, nor have I started any unwanted fires, but use common sense and be aware of your surroundings.

2 | For wood-only fire, use a knife or small axe to split wood into smaller and smaller strips. Gather them around a few balled-up pieces of newspaper. Or gather small twigs and sticks, and pile them over some birch bark. Ignite

the materials, and then slowly add larger and larger pieces of wood. Note that for direct grilling over a wood fire you will need to wait until you are left with only coals. Cooking over large flames will blacken your meat with creosote, which will result in epic failure.

3 | The best of both worlds is to start with coal in the chimney and remove some coals before they are ready. Carefully peeking into the chimney, you should be able to see lots of bright-red embers—not all of the coal will be engulfed in flames. At this point I dump some of the coals out of the chimney into a pile on one side of the grill and add a few wood chunks. After 10 minutes, the coals should be covered with ash, and there should

be no high flames. Regardless of the fuel I am using, it's good to get the cooking grates over the coals as soon as possible to get them blistering hot before adding food.

4 | If your cooking grates are thin and spaghetti-like in diameter, you will be ready to add food more quickly than you would with heavy cast iron grates, which will take a few minutes to get hot. While the grates are heating up, get a sense of how hot your fire actually is.

5 | I put my hand 6 inches over the grill at its hottest area to see how long I can keep it there. Two seconds means the grill is too hot! Meat will burn within 30 seconds at this high temperature, which is only good for thin steaks that you want to have raw in the middle. At 4 seconds the temperature is ideal for red meat, steaks, burgers, lamb, and the like. Meat at this medium heat will begin to burn in about 5 minutes; that's generally sufficient time for each side of a steak to get a great crust. For somewhat more delicate pork and veal, 6 seconds is great. This medium-low temperature is also great for cooking sturdy fish such as tuna, swordfish, and salmon. At 8 seconds the temperature is ideal for cooking chicken, sausages, and more delicate fish. See the next page for a summation of grill temperatures and timing with a hand check.

DETERMINING GRILL TEMPERATURE BY HAND (POSITIONED 6 INCHES ABOVE THE GRILL)

TEMPERATURE	THERMOMETER READING	HAND CHECK
High	450°F–500°F	2 seconds
Medium-High	400°F–450°F	3 seconds
Medium	350°F–400°F	4 seconds
Medium-Low	300°F–350°F	6–7 seconds
Low	250°F–300°F	8 seconds

THOUGH I RESPECT LONG-SLEEVED, POLYESTER, DISCO SHIRTS, WHEN YOU'RE CHECKING GRILL TEMPERATURES, IT'S A TERRIBLE TIME TO BE WEARING THEM!

INDIRECT GRILLING

Any food placed on the grill that is not directly above burning coals would be considered indirect grilling. The range of possible temperatures depends greatly on the size and shape of the grill, the amount of fuel, and whether or not the grill's lid is closed. I find that round grills like Weber Kettles and Big Green Eggs distribute heat very well to indirect areas because of their shape; a square box grill, much less so. Grilling food somewhat quickly with indirect heat would be considered barbecue cooking, and grilling food very slowly with low heat and a wood fuel would be considered smoking. So technically, anytime you grill and have at least some wood as fuel and close the lid, you are also barbecuing and smoking.

CHARCOAL BRIQUETTES AND LUMP CHARCOAL: TO USE OR NOT TO USE?

I tend not to add charcoal briquettes while cooking food. "Instant light" ones, soaked in chemicals, will become engulfed in flames, which drastically raises temperatures and adds a terrible taste. Untreated briquettes are made with lime and starch. (The lime makes the briquettes turn ash-white while they are burning to indicate that it's time to throw the food on.) These briquettes take a long time to get hot and block heat while doing so, which will throw off your game.

On the other hand, I don't mind adding lump charcoal to a fire while the food is cooking. It has fewer chemicals than briquettes, ignites very quickly, and doesn't block heat (as briquettes do) because of its irregular and stick shaped.

The great thing about having a chimney for a starter is you can get coals of any source going on the side and add hot ones in when they're ready. The downside to this is you will need to remove all food and grates while adding the flaming pile of coals and readjust the placement of the food while getting your temperature right.

ADVANTAGES OF COOKING OVER INDIRECT HEAT

Making the decision to cook over direct or indirect heat comes down to how hot you need the grill to be, depending on what you're cooking. Grill temperatures rise and fall, often precipitously, so your goal is to keep the fire consistent, understand the lifespan of the fire, and cook accordingly. The fire temp will peak after about an hour with briquettes and then slowly cool down. Lump coal will reach top heat in 30 minutes but will then die down fast—making it ideal for a nice steak. A whole chicken needs a good hour at a medium-high temperature (400°F). A hotter temperature will burn the skin before the inside of the bird is thoroughly cooked. A cooler fire will require too much time for it to cook on the grill and to get the skin right—and the moisture will be long gone before the chicken is safe to eat. Chicken and fish are great for indirect grilling, and it's the perfect method for finishing off fat steaks and chops, when their crusts have already reached perfection, but the interior still needs some cooking. And remember, the longer you cook food over indirect heat, the more time it has to absorb flavor from the wood.

GRILLS

To be honest I have never used a gas grill. Not even once. Though apparently they are more convenient, I can't help but always think I will blow myself up, which ultimately makes these grills much less convenient for me. I have a couple of Brinkmann® barrel smokers that I use to grill when I'm not smoking ribs. I also have two mini Weber grills that are great for smaller meals; both are inexpensive and convenient, especially for strict vegetarian guests who simply cannot eat food that has been cooked on the same grill as meat. I'll assure them that one of them is my kosher "veggie" grill. I always forget which one!

I like all grills and think folks should just follow their guts and budget when it comes to buying one. A large, classic Weber grill with a little flip-up grate that allows you to tinker with the coals without lifting off the grate is efficient, is large enough to cook more food (than the minis), and is grill master–tested and approved. The $20 square-ish grills purchased from discount stores also work, though they are not very deep, which makes controlling temperatures more difficult. They are also wobbly and will show all your friends and in-laws that you're way out of your element. I really like the grills that have a crank arm, so you can raise and lower the coal bed to control the temperature. Most Walmart® stores sell a version of this crank-armed grill, and although it is made from low-grade metal and has plastic wheels, it'll last several years and will only set you back about $120. Again, I've not had any experience with gas grills, but then you don't really need experience to operate one. You can add wood chunks in a small metal smoke box to impart great flavors to whatever you're grilling, and they also allow for flare-ups from sizzling juices that lend great flavor to food.

ALL THE RECIPES IN THIS BOOK CAN BE DONE ON A GAS GRILL.

Barrel-shaped grills and smokers are great because the cooking surface is rectangular, making it easy to have plenty of indirect cooking space. They also tend to have a built-in thermometer, which is great for getting a sense of the grill's inner temperature. Circular grills, because of their shape, can get very hot with less fuel, and you can make a small wood fire and get a considerable amount of usable, indirect space. To achieve more indirect cooking area in your grill, consider using a barrier of some kind to allow plenty of fuel for high temperatures but little direct flame-to-meat contact. The plate-like base of a clay pot is great for this, as it's thin and wide and holds and conducts heat well. An alternate is to use a heavy-duty foil tray. You can add a little water for moisture or a bunch of crushed garlic and herbs to your grill to generate flavorful smoke. You can also block the direct power of the flames by placing food on a fancy cedar plank or on sliced fruits and vegetables, such as lemons, oranges, and apples. These sacrificial fruits and vegetables will impart delicate flavors, moisture, and protection before being easily shoved into the flames. Empty sardine cans, preferably filled with water, herbs, or flavorful sauces, can be fashioned as a bed as well. At the end of the day, you can grill in a smoker and smoke in a griller—even a small one—with glorious success.

When shopping for a grill, consider how many people you will be cooking for, how often you cook, and of course how much you want to spend. Cheap grills are disposable; full-size grills are durable and reliable; and quality, metal-drum grills command attention and create a sense of pride.

Here are some of the options:

Hibachi. Basically a flowerpot with some coals at the bottom and some skewers sitting over the top.

Yakitori. Similar to a hibachi, the design of this grill is long and rectangular in order to accommodate lots of skewers, all running parallel.

Mini Weber. An expensive version of the flowerpot, it has a lid, vents, handles, and so on, so you have a grill, not a flowerpot.

99-cent store grill. This $20 boxy grill is cheap, wobbly, and very shallow, both physically and personality-wise. But dang it, it does the trick in a pinch. Try to find a small prop to get the grill a little higher off the coals.

Weber. This grill is classic, efficient, and circular.

Big Green Egg. This grill is expensive, heavy, and heat radiating. It is the Le Creuset® of grills.

Adjustable grill. An awesome no-frills grill. You can raise and lower the grill without having to move food or obsessively maintain the coals.

Barrel grill. This type affords tons of grilling space for direct grilling, as well as room to cook with indirect heat. You can make a fire on one side and place meat on the other. It is efficient for smoking smaller batches of meat.

Barrel grill with offset smoker. This type provides lots of real estate for either direct or indirect grilling. With the fire contained in a separate place, specifically for smoking, it provides more consistent heat and more space, and you don't have to open the grill door.

Gas grill. This type is becoming more and more like a stainless steel outdoor kitchen, complete with separate cooking station, rotisserie, shelving, and perhaps a handy-dandy bottle opener. It's easy to get going and maintain a steady temperature with this grill.

FUEL

Growing up in New Hampshire 30 years ago, I remember the winters. They were cold, dark, and long. Temperatures would often sink to twenty below zero. Everything was frozen stiff, and even the smoke from the chimney rose straight into the sky like a stalagmite. The basement of our farmhouse held two cords of wood that fed the cast-iron stoves. To sit at night, hearing the coyotes in the distance and staring into the flames . . . feeling the radiating heat across your face, this love has been with us since we first harnessed fire. It has cooked our food, given us light, kept us warm, and most importantly, it has kept us safe from predators. Grilling with wood and coal imparts deep, complex flavors into the food. It is no wonder that fire still brings us so much peace and tranquility.

Humans have used many materials for creating fire, but certain ones work best for grilling.

BRIQUETTES VS. LUMP CHARCOAL

Briquettes. This type of fuel burns very steadily for a long time and is easy to find at most stores. Instant-light charcoal briquettes are available. A big pile of these is a cinch to ignite; however, the instant-lights do take a good 30 minutes to get up to temperature. Because even non-instant-light briquettes have some chemicals, new ones should not be thrown in while the cooking is underway. Instant-light briquettes will leave your grill (and possibly your food) smelling of chemicals. Adding some of these to an existing fire is like cooking with plastic—an ill-advised thing to do.

Lump charcoal. This stuff can spark a lot, and buying it can be frustrating because you won't get a bunch of even-sized briquettes. Sometimes chunks can be annoyingly huge on one end and a fine powder on the other. But, for me at least, they are superior in every other way to briquettes. They light easily and come up to heat very quickly. They also burn very hot, which means you can use less of them. But what is crucial for me is that with natural lump charcoal, you can add more to your fire as you cook. Lump charcoal doesn't have chemicals like briquettes, and because of the small pieces in the bag, you can add little bits as you go and not disrupt the cooking.

WOOD FOR THE GRILL

Wood chips. Wood chips are nice to add to the grill to impart a bit flavor. They are readily available in many stores, and it's easy to find all kinds of wood types that may not grow naturally where you live. They burn very quickly and are best suited for quick cooks.

Wood chunks. These are also easy to find in many stores and in many varieties. Wood chunks are generally large enough to burn for 30 minutes or so. Because of their shapes, they don't normally create as much flame as, say, a stick would. This means you won't have

as drastic a spike in temperature and instead can smoke for longer, which imparts good flavors.

Wood logs. A single wood log can be equal to several bags of chunks or chips, and in its full size, will burn for hours, imparting great flavor to whatever you're cooking. Wood logs are generally used in large smokers for big cuts of meat that may take hours or days to cook. But I also love them for grilling. Pound for pound they are they cheapest way to get wood on the fire, and with a little work, they are easily split and made into small chunks and chips. Obviously, this type of fuel is not for everyone, but if you have access to good hardwood logs and a saw or an axe, you can turn a large log into any size and shape you like. Also note that a smaller log can easily be split by standing it upright and then using a sturdy outdoor knife to hammer it through with another log. This is a classic technique for outdoors folks that can easily be applied to the backyard.

Wood sticks. Sticks are easy to find, impart good smoke flavors, don't require carpentry, and are free! It's good to know, however, what kind of wood you are using. For example, you want to avoid pine and birch, as they make for a sooty fire. Hickory and oak sticks, on the other hand, are grilling gold.

TYPES OF WOOD

Living in Brooklyn for 15 years, I was limited to the kind of wood I could get. Birch and oak are sold as firewood at bodegas and hardware stores. **Birch** is very light and dry and easy to make small, quick fires. Dainty sheets of peeled bark can be used to start the fire and work better than newspaper. Regardless, they don't have much flavor, and all bark must be removed from birch, as an oil resin in the bark will burn and ruin food, as well as leave a unique smell in your grill for some time to come. **Oak** adds good, smoky flavor. It is also very hard and dense and burns a long time, making it great for long-cooking items like ribs or smoking brisket. Its flavor is medium, making it one of the most popular woods for grilling.

Whenever family would visit from Vermont or New Hampshire, they would bring some **apple wood**, and I would use it whenever I could. It

has what I would describe as a light and delicate flavor. It's easy to like.

Mesquite brings a heavy and intense smoke flavor that is too strong for most applications. It's most popular in Texas for smoking brisket. **Hickory** is my favorite wood for cooking. It's got big, complex flavor, but is not overwhelming, and it applies well to a range of foods,

MANAGING THE FIRE

When I am grilling for a lot of people, several courses go on and off the grill. Generally, lighting up a big pile of coals results in a very hot fire that eventually tapers off. And usually the things I like to cook first—chicken wings, corn and other veggies, and sauces—don't do well with high heat. So I start a medium-sized coal fire in a chimney with a fire starter, using either briquettes or larger chunks of lump charcoal from the bag. Once most of the coals are glowing, I pour them out into a pile in my grill. After 10 minutes or so, the grill is all warmed up, and radiating heat, not a super-blistering fire. In fact, when I spread out the pile of coals, the direct heat areas are just right for appetizers and/or foods that take a bit more time to cook with less heat. I'll then add a chuck of wood to the fire to start getting the benefit of those flavors as well. From this point on, I manage the heat by adding smaller lump pieces. With enough of them, I can keep the grill at a steady temperature all night. I always have wood on hand to keep the smoke going, and, if I need to pop up the heat a bit quickly, I can add some sticks or chips that light up right away and can quickly raise temperatures. As the meal progresses, maybe you come up to the final course of either steak or fish. Both of these require way high temperatures, plus possible a lower temp area to rest or cook thoroughly after a good sear. This can be done slowly by adding more and more lump charcoal, until the heat gets intense, or you can get another chimney of coal going on the side, and dump the coals in exactly when you want them. It's a choreography that requires a bit of forethought and a good understanding of your grill and food. And though the show may not go off without a hitch every time, when it does, it is a sight to behold.

MAINTAINING YOUR GRILL

If you buy a quality, heavy, steel grill (Brinkmann® makes some heavy suckers with cast iron wagon wheels), you can expect it to last many, many years. Covers make sense for gas grills to protect all the fancy technological wizardry. Good-quality, heavy iron grills take a long time to cool down and fill with ash as they cool, which should be removed before covering or storing.

I find that wiping down the outside of my grill once in a while with some oil keeps it in good condition and delays rusting. Just make sure that the lid is closed and all ash is removed if the grill is going to be exposed to rain and other elements. Wet ash will rust out your grill VERY fast.

I always break in a new grill by making a raging fire inside of it, letting it go for a couple hours, and then allowing it to cool down. This will burn out any residual chemicals. As long as you don't use instant-light charcoal, burn any birch bark, or use weird oils, your grill will begin to take on a great smell after you cook just a couple of fatty cuts of meat. In time, a thin, burnt crust of fats, ash, and creosote will develop around the top and edges of the grill. This stuff can begin to fall off the lid when you close it or end up on your food, which you do not want to happen. So keep an eye on that buildup and clean it off from time to time with a wire brush to avoid those nasty mishaps.

GRILLING OVER A CAMPFIRE

Rather than lobotomizing my sweet children with screen-based entertainment, I encourage them to do what ALL children in the history of our planet have done, up until, literally, just a few years ago—go outside. We rummage around for sticks, make a little teepee fire, and roast marshmallows. Sometimes we roast a chicken on a spit. Mateo and Zoe become enthralled with nature up close. During these times around the fire, we discuss the deepest mysteries of the cosmos: "Can

salamanders swim?" "Why is fire yellow?" "Could Shredder from *TMNT* really exist?" As I attempt to navigate these questions, with the mastery befitting my station, I realize that the *only* question they ask me, when in front of a screen, is "What is your password?"

Anyone who has attempted to do a rotisserie in the woods knows that you cannot simply impale a chicken or lamb leg with a stick and cook it like a marshmallow. The stick can break, or if you don't insert it properly, the stick can spin in place, rather than rotating the meat over the

fire. And steaks can cook unevenly if they aren't spread out in the right way. Below are a few techniques for making spits, stands, and grills out of wood and other natural elements.

Rotisserie #1: For birds and small legs. Cut a fresh sapling or branch that is about 1 inch thick and 5 feet long. Fashion both ends of the stick into points. While doing this, keep a thin, 5- to 6-inch-long shaving that is still thick enough to be stiff. With an axe or a knife, make a small split in the stick where you want the bird to be. I make it between the middle of the stick and one pointy end. Insert the thin, wood shaving into the split and work it through, so that it is centered. When attaching the chicken, angle the shaving as much as possible so that the

chicken can slide around it. Then straighten out the crossbar so that it's flat and perpendicular to the main shaft (the stick). The crossbar, if it's sturdy and long enough, will firmly hold the chicken in place. Then, jamb the far, pointed end of the stick into the dirt at an angle so that it hangs over the fire. A rock or two can help keep it at a good angle.

Rotisserie #2: For legs and steaks. Find a fresh sapling or branch that is small enough to stab the meat but big enough to support it. The sapling should have a fork in it, and both prongs of the fork should be as parallel as possible. With a knife or an axe, take the forked end pieces and whittle them down so they are thin, smooth, and pointy. Piercing the meat with both prongs will keep it from spinning. If you're cooking a steak, the fork should be wide enough to keep the steak fanned out, not sagging. Sharpen the other end of the branch, and stab it into the ground.

Rotisserie #3: For heavy meats like pork shoulder, brisket, or whole pigs (under 50 pounds). Follow the steps for Rotisserie #2 but make two spits. Also make sure each spit is strong enough to support at least half the weight of the meat. The forked prongs should also be long enough to penetrate at least halfway through the meat. Insert each stick into the meat from opposite ends to create a rotisserie. Use other sticks or rocks as supports to position the spit at the correct height over the fire. Note that most big cuts like a good searing, but they also need longer indirect heat for some if not most of their cook. Since being on a spit leaves the meat exposed and prone to drying out (especially since you've stabbed holes in it with sticks), wrapping it up in tinfoil is a good solution.

Shawarma. Using a stick of bamboo or other kind of thin but sturdy and smooth stick that is a few feet long, follow the steps for Rotisserie #1. Spread the crossbar out so it is perpendicular to the main shaft. Using a slice of pineapple or watermelon rind, gently stab the spit through the center and slide it down until it rests on the crossbar. Thinly sliced, marinated meat can be stacked on top of the pineapple (or watermelon rind) and placed next to the source of heat.

Pine grill: For steaks, chops, or fish. Gather about twenty small fan-shaped pine branches with lots of needles. Separate these into two equal-sized piles and arrange each into a thick, interwoven bunch that can support the food you want to cook. On the first pile, lay your food on top and place it atop a bed of coals. The main purpose of the pine needles is to keep your food from lying directly in the coals. The branches should be sturdy enough to survive over a hot fire for 5 minutes (for steaks or chops), or a medium-hot fire for 7 minutes (for fish). Lay the steaks, chops, or fish on one pine grill, and cook the meat on one side. Then transfer the meat to a second pine grill, and cook it on the other side.

TOOLS

Knife. Anyone who loves to cook inevitably realizes they need a good sharp, well-maintained knife. This is crucial. If I could have just one knife, it would be an old-school cleaver—the kind

that has a pointy tip, as opposed to a flat end. Cleavers are big and durable, and they can do many tasks, including prying up grill grates and chopping up small chunks of wood. I also really love a low-cost, curved butchering blade. This knife is flexible and good for breaking down meat with bones, such as chickens and chops.

Though I have an extensive collection of knives, including handmade, high-carbon, folded-steel masterpieces from Seki, Japan, with cocobolo wood handles and gorgeous brass rivets, they are too delicate and ornate and, though razor sharp, can be brittle and not great around bones, metal, and fire.

Mortar and pestle. I use these tools for every single meal. Why? Because they do it all! For example, I keep glass canning jars full of different peppercorns from around the world, jars of different salts, dried chile peppers, allspice, nutmeg, herbs, and so forth. All I have to do is grab a handful of any of those ingredients, throw it in the stone bowl, and grind away until it's the size I want. Fine powders are great for baking, but for big meats and fire, you want larger chunks. I can do this on the fly with my mortar and pestle and with any combination of ingredients. Try doing that with a pepper grinder! Also these tools are really just two rocks. It doesn't get any more beautiful or simple than that. I once saw my 12-year-old niece in Cameroon make a salsa with just two smooth stones; one flatter and one rounder. She crushed garlic, then added herbs, peppers, and parsley and, with a beautiful circular motion, turned the stuff into a puree. It took her literally 3 minutes to make it, and then she wiped it off into a bowl. When I asked why she didn't prefer using a food processor or a blender, she matter-of-factly replied that they were a pain to wash. Two stones, on the other hand, have no intricate moving parts or multiple pieces to be bothered by!

Charcoal chimney. Every barbecue section of every store in the United States should have one—a metal cylinder with a handle. There is a

little piece of metal that separates the top two-thirds of the chimney from the bottom third. To get it going, dump some coal or wood chunks into the top part and wad some newspaper into the bottom. Light the newspaper without any chemical accelerants, and watch how the heat rises and burns the coals. As the heat increases, the flow of air that is sucked in increases as well. It's like a blowtorch and will get your fuel going fast. What's best is that you can then pour out the fuel in any way you fancy. It's also great to get a side order of burning coals going in the chimney while grilling is under way. Leaving coals in the chimney will produce an extremely hot fire. That fire can be kept burning on its own and used to caramelize glazes or for a touch-up on the crust before serving.

I don't burn myself. Also, watch out for some tongs that have sharp corners—they can tear at delicate foods like chicken and fish. Others tongs are smooth and have more rounded edges, but this can make it more difficult to actually grab things. Lately, instead of tongs, I've been using long chopsticks, the kind that Japanese udon masters use to handle noodles. I figure if a guy is able to grab hold of a wet noodle with chopsticks, I should be able to grab a chicken wing with them. Cons: Chopsticks, since they are made of wood, will indeed catch fire and can cross-contaminate raw food because they can't be cleaned with fire. For spatulas, I really like the cheap kind, made of very thin metal. They're great for sliding under delicate meats.

Cast iron pans. Although they are not a requirement for grilling, these tough pans are great to keep sauces simmering alongside meat as you're grilling it. I often keep a pan going with a mix of honey, canola oil, and salt—a glaze that I use to paint on meats before presenting them. You can get cast iron pans in sizes ranging from as small as a hockey puck to much larger ones; the choice of which to use depends on what you are cooking. Cast iron pans have no meltable parts, and some are sold with a lid, which is great for baking biscuits alongside your favorite grilled chicken or shrimp dish.

Tongs and spatulas. These tools are crucial, but it really makes a difference to use the right ones for whatever the job happens to be. Some tongs and spatulas are very short, for example, which means that the long-sleeved, fancy, polyester shirt you're wearing might become part of the meal. I like longer tools so

OPTIONAL TOOLS

Meat grinder. If you like taking matters into your own hands, grinding meat is especially rewarding. Where some upstanding citizens have a delightful little juicer, you, my friend, have a solid steel meat grinder gracing the end of your countertop. Buying fancy ground beef and sausages costs way more than making your own at home in 2 seconds, and you get to be the creator! Even if you never use the thing, having a cast iron $20 grinder somewhere in your arsenal sure lets people know that you aren't playing around.

Metal wire. Be careful NOT to use galvanized steel for any cooking endeavor. Stainless steel wire is easy to find and is good for attaching chicken and large legs to spits.

Rosemary or thyme bundles. Tied up to use as a brush, these fragrant bundles come in handy.

Empty sardine cans. Fill one of these cans with the liquid of your choice and simply place it under meat that requires a longer cooking time.

THE IMPORTANCE OF USING QUALITY MEAT

If you don't hunt for your own meat, it comes from one of two places: a nearby family farm, where the folks live off slim margins but care about their trade and are proud of their product, and where the livestock is fed natural foods and allowed to socialize and graze and live well—just as in a kids' books—or it comes from the billion-dollar meat industry. It should go without saying that the meat industry is basically something straight out of a dystopian horror film. By its own account, the meat industry is doing "a great job!" selling billions of pounds of meat every year, just in the United States, not to mention the over 1 million metric tons of beef we export to our carnivorous friends and neighbors. Business is booming!

Raised in the dark with no room to move, on a diet of growth hormones and antibiotics, and suffering from fecal burns, humungous, gluttonous chickens are ready for slaughter just a month and a half after birth. Feedlot cattle and pork are crammed, abused, and confined for life, raised on corn, and also fed hormones, of course. Once again, truth is scarier than fiction. Corn is used as feed because it's cheap and makes cows fat fast, but it results in meat with a poor flavor. To make matters worse, hormone injections cause cows to gain water weight, which also reduces the flavor and tenderness of beef. This is not to say you can't get prime-grade beef that has great marbling, but it doesn't mean it has any great flavor.

Today, our markets are flooded with cheap, grain-fed cattle, of which each of us devours roughly 9 ounces (the equivalent of two huge hamburgers!) every waking day. And how do those get-fat-fast hormones end up? Slathered in ketchup and mustard and chowed down by us!

On the other hand, the meat we get from animals that we allow to live like animals that eat real diets of quality food, and that are not traumatized every waking second of life are far more delicious and tender and have deeper flavor. Aaron Franklin, owner of what is considered the best barbecue place in the United States, only sources the finest meat available. People like Aaron Franklin are not just ignoring mass-produced corn-fed cattle out of moral principal (though it's more than enough reason to do so), they are doing it because they actually care how food tastes—and they know that the way to get that great flavor begins with the best ingredients: happy, grass-fed cattle. These animals don't grow as large or as quickly as do cattle that are fed hormones; therefore, the meat from these creatures costs more, especially if beef is dry-aged for 40 days and loses even more weight to evaporation. But the end product is completely different. The umami flavor of the beef intensifies with the number of days it is aged, until you're eating something so rich, so complex, so tender that it has almost no relationship to the same cow that was rushed through the feedlot. It might cost twice as much, pound for pound, as other meats, but it is twice as rich, will go twice as far, and it will be twice as filling—with the same number of calories!

The other benefit of not supporting the industrial meat fiasco is the support you give to a local business run by someone who actually cares about producing quality meat from healthy animals that are humanely raised and slaughtered. There's nothing quite like "nerding out" with a meat monger to gain some serious chops about chops. They can show you features of meat that you may have never considered before, such as grain, fat, and tenderness. Soon you can request cuts down to the very specifics, like the exact part of the short ribs you want. In the end, if you fancy yourself a grill master, shopping around for quality meat and vendors is crucial.

2

BURGERS

As a nation of burger lovers, our freedom of expression is practiced one burger at a time: sizzling tender ground beef, paired with crispy lettuce, creamy sauces, and sweet pickles—an American classic, and arguably the perfect food. The burger is perfect because of the pure genius of its design. Every component can be tasted simultaneously and doesn't even require a fork to eat. A single bite can provide all the satisfaction, nutrition, and joy of an entire meal.

Whereas some people have a doctorate in quantum mathematics or string theory, I have spent a heck of a lot of time tinkering with burgers. To me the burger is the greatest food because it is more than the sum of its parts: the combination of sweet, sour, salty, umami, creamy condiments, and soft dough all come together in perfect harmony.

There are purists, of course, those who believe in only the bare necessities—meat, bread, and maybe cheese. Folks, I salute you, for every one of us is an equal authority on the matter of what a burger is and should be. And I agree that many burgers have gotten completely out of hand.

The amount of stuff people try to shove into a single burger does injustice to its portability and ergonomics. And then there is also the bacon bandage Yes, the bun may suck, the meat may be dry, and the cheese might not be melted properly, but wait! The addition of bacon somehow atones for these reckless, carnal sins. But not all sins are quite as obscene. There is, for example, the subtle misdeed of going too big on the bun. The latest fad is layering your prized jowl, marrow, and *fois gras* in a brioche bun. These constructions can be 4 inches high, naked, and often showing signs of staleness. What happened to balance and harmony? For me the perfect burger starts with the perfect bun. I find the best and easiest way to get perfection is to modify store-bought ones (see page 28 for more information).

One of the misconceptions about the hamburger is that it was brought from Germany, whereas in actuality it is a completely American creation. People have been serving meat on bread since the 1700s, but the burger, as we know it, didn't have an identity and mass acknowledgment in the United States until the 1920s, when Billy Ingram created White Castle, his burger restaurant chain. In 1954, when Ray Kroc joined McDonald's, he took what Ingram had

started to the next level. The ubiquitous presence along the highways of burger joints such as McDonald's and Burger King coincided with the great postwar expansion of America. Freedom and mobility—the burger was the food that came with all that. And though the hamburger drive-through was made possible by Eisenhower's highways, couldn't we argue that it was the other way around?

As the winner of Esquire TV's *The Next Great Burger*, I'm ready to lead the charge in helping burger lovers, home cooks, and even advanced chefs discover the rewards of experimentation and creative flavor combinations. For *The Next Great Burger* competition, I took inspiration from the classic Louisiana treat, the beignet, to create a unique hamburger bun. A beignet is a savory doughnut, deep-fried for a crispy outer shell and a soft dough interior. It's a beauty to look at and provides texture beyond the call of duty. I chose it, however, because a good beignet needs something sweet to compliment it. At Cafe Du Monde® in New Orleans, they are doused with powdered sugar and served with chicory coffee. My winning burger called for a handsome dollop of pear jelly at the bottom and a creamy aioli on the top.

CLASSIC BURGER

Let's start at the beginning. The only thing required in a burger is a patty and a bun. This quintessential combo however has little room for error. This is half the reason people add all the other stuff. The fundamentals were not right. It's all distraction. The beef must be flavorful and heavy on the fat content. I love the flavor of grass-fed and grass-finished beef, but it runs low on fat, so adding some additional fat is required. The bun must be soft, light, and crispy, and it must contain enough texture to absorb the juices. Only large, flaky salt should be used, as it provides texture at this size.

For the basic burger, I prefer a 3.5-ounce patty, about the size of a jumbo egg. The meat does not have to be from choice cuts but rather can be from a good mix of flavorful beef and fat. Meat from Angus cattle, for example, is known for its rich flavor. This can be a good option, or, if you're grinding it yourself, skirt, hangar, and sirloin steak are great candidates. Use a blend with at least 20 percent fat. If you go higher than 20 percent, start with a larger patty, as much of the size will reduce when cooking.

> MAKES 4 BURGERS

1 pound 80/20 ground beef

4 enriched burger buns

Salt, coarse or flake

1. Start a charcoal or wood fire. Let it burn down to embers and until the temperature is medium high.

2. While the meat is still cold, shape it into five patties, each ½ inch thick. They do not need to be perfectly round (pottery skills are not required). Odd shapes are fine and leave little ridges that get a little burnt and crispy.

3. Get the coals blazing to medium-high heat.

4. Examining your patties, make sure that the buns have a slightly smaller diameter and that each side of the bun is the same thickness as the patties. The patties will shrink during cooking. The amount depends on how much fat content is in your meat.

5. Lightly, but thoroughly, butter each side of the buns.

6. Pat down the patties to dry, then add a pinch of salt to each side of the burgers. Place them on the grill.

7. Grill the patties for 2 to 3 minutes or until the bottoms are a crunchy dark brown. Flip the burgers. Grill on the other side for 2 more minutes, or until blood appears on the top of the patty, for a rare burger. Add an extra minute or so for each stage of doneness. Remove the patties from the grill, plate them, and let them rest.

(continued on page 28)

8. Lay the buns on indirect heat, and cover them with tinfoil, a metal lid, or a bowl. Ideally, buns should be soft and steamy with the buttered bottoms a golden crispy brown. If buns are steamy but not yet crispy on the bottom, move them to a higher-heat area. If the opposite is true, move them to lower heat.

9. Stack the buns with the patties, and serve with the condiments of your choice—lettuce, tomatoes, onions, pickles . . . the list of burger add-ons is endless.

DEEP THOUGHTS ON BUNS

The bun is the most visible element of the burger. It is the first thing you touch. And, unlike every other ingredient in a burger, it must contain two parts in every bite: the top and bottom. It's kind of a big deal. You don't have to make your own to have the perfect bun. The best I have ever had, except for my deep-fried beignet, is a modified store-bought one. Here are some tips: Potato rolls have the perfect density and softness. They are a no-brainer in most situations; yet they are made from potatoes and have a unique flavor, which, to my mind, is great for brisket and pulled pork, but is not ideal for burgers.

I prefer an enriched white bun with a similar density. Most store-bought enriched hamburger buns are on the dry side. A simple test is to pick up the bag of buns. Does it have a little weight, or is it feather light? If you press one of the buns with your thumb, does it stay pressed or instantly bounce back into shape? Quality buns have more weight and don't instantly rebound from a press. The last thing you want is a cheap crumbly bun, but one can be modified in a pinch. Simply melt some butter and paint it generously on each side of the bun before adding it to the grill. Doing so will add more fat and moisture, which is a good thing, of course.

Also, using the whole bun can result in a grossly disproportioned hamburger, which is clearly unacceptable. Are you serving some nice meats and flavors inside a bun or are you serving a bun with some flavors inside? Don't hesitate to take that store-bought bun and trim out a little from the middle. I do this 80 percent of the time.

CHEESE-STUFFED MEATBALL SLIDERS WITH WHISKEY SAUCE

Few things are as rewarding as stuffing little cheese cubes into balls of meat and drizzling sweet whiskey all over them.

Whiskey Sauce (see recipe on page 169)

1 pound 80/20 ground beef

1/4 pound cheese, cubed; preferably one that melts really well, like cheddar, pepper jack, Brie, or such

Salt, coarse or flake

8 potato slider buns or enriched white slider buns.

1. Prepare the Whiskey Sauce in advance. Set aside.

2. To prepare the meat, shape it into 3-ounce balls (about the size of an egg).

3. Press your thumb into each ball to make a deep pouch.

4. Add a cube of cheese to each ball, and seal with meat. Try to make meat thickness as even as possible. Press gently to resemble a fat patty.

5. Sprinkle the meatballs with salt.

6. Bring the grill to medium-high heat. Then place the meatballs on the grill, and cook on each side for 1 minute.

7. The sliders are done when the cheese begins to melt out.

8. Add the buns facedown on indirect heat, and cover to steam.

9. Serve with Whiskey Sauce.

BEIGNET CLASSIC BURGER

When I was first asked to compete in *The Next Great Burger*, a great sense of dread consumed me. It wasn't competing or having to grill 75 burgers in an hour for a hungry TV audience that was stressing me out. It was the idea that I might have to bake that terrified me—all those little, precise measurements, uncooperative yeast, kneading, resting, repeating. And all of that for what? To still screw it up in the end! No, I couldn't bare the agony!

This is the recipe I made up and that ultimately won Esquire's *The Next Great Burger* contest. It's complicated but only because it is composed of several techniques: making deep-fried beignets, making pickles, two sauces, a rub, and, of course, grilling. But once each process is learned, it can be used for other applications.

> MAKES 8 BURGERS

Lex's Pasilla Salt (page 141)

Beignets (page 172)

Pear Jelly (page 185)

Lex's Pickles (page 183), or use store-bought, such as McClure's™

Saffron Aioli (page 165)

Saffron Oil (page 165)

2 pounds 80/20 ground Wagyu beef (4 ounces per patty)

8 slices aged Vermont cheddar (1 slice per burger)

2 large heirloom tomatoes, sliced ¼-inch thick

1 large red onion, sliced very thin

1 cup baby arugula leaves (about 5 leaves per burger)

1. Prepare the Lex's Pasilla Salt, Beignets, Pear Jelly, Lex's Pickles, Saffron Aioli, and Saffron Oil in advance, and set aside until ready for use.

2. Preheat the grill to medium-high.

3. Form the beef into eight 4-ounce patties, about ½ inch thick. Season each with just a pinch of Lex's Pasilla Salt.

4. Oil the grill, and make sure each patty has even, direct heat under it. Grill each patty on one side for 3 minutes. With a spatula, gently flip the patty, layer on one or two slices of cheese, and cover. Cook for another 3 minutes.

5. The cheese should be melted and gooey. Remove the patties and set them aside.

6. Build the burgers from the bottom of the beignet up with:

1½ tablespoons Pear Jelly

Red onion

Lex's Pickles slices

Beef patty with melted slice of cheese

Lex's Pasilla Salt (a generous dose)

Arugula

Heirloom tomato

Beignet top, smeared with 1 tablespoon Saffron Aioli

> DEPENDING ON THE ACIDITY OR SWEETNESS OF THE PICKLES, KETCHUP MAY BE ADDED TO BALANCE OUT THE SWEET/SOUR ELEMENT.

MUSHROOM BURGER

I started this recipe using lobster mushrooms. They are impressive! Not only are they dense and rich, with hints of seafood, they are also a bit uncommon and look great as a menu item. But in the end, the affordable, ubiquitous portobello was just plain tastier. The first time I tried this recipe, I got goose bumps all over. It is that good! At events, I serve these burgers on a deep-fried beignet, as I do for most of my burgers, but they are also delectable on a properly buttered and grilled store-bought bun.

▶ MAKES 6 BURGERS ◀

½ cup Heirloom Pico de Gallo (page 159)

2 large portobello mushrooms, sliced

3 tablespoons olive oil

Salt

1½ cups Queso Oaxaca or mozzarella cheese, shredded

6 white buns, buttered and lightly toasted or grilled

1. Prepare Pico de Gallo, and set the mixture aside until ready to assemble sandwiches.

2. Slice mushrooms into ¼-inch strips, and mix in oil and salt.

3. Grill the mushroom strips over medium heat for 2 minutes per side.

4. Place mushroom slices next to each other on the grill, to make a bed, and cover it loosely with the shredded cheese. Cover the mushroom slices with lid.

5. When the cheese has melted, serve the mushrooms, with a heaping spoonful of Pico de Gallo, on a bun.

SHRIMP BURGER

This shrimp "burger" can be made with shrimp of any size. I don't even make patties. I just butterfly, dry rub, and flash-grill the shrimp. Served on a beignet bun, it is godly; although it is perfectly good on a buttered and grilled white bun too. The smoky spiciness of the pasilla peppers in the rub complements the sweet mango very well, and the Coconut Curry Sauce adds a warm, rich, and healthy element that ties everything together. Cilantro adds fresh greens and works well off the curry flavor.

MAKES 6 BURGERS

Lex's Pasilla Salt (page 141)

1½ cups Coconut Curry Sauce, divided use (page 155)

2 tablespoons soft unsalted butter

6 hamburger buns

1 pound peeled shrimp

1 ripe mango, cut into 18 very thin slices

¼ cup loosely chopped cilantro

1. Prepare Lex's Pasilla Salt and the Coconut Curry Sauce, and set the mixtures aside until ready for use.

2. Bring the grill to medium-high heat.

3. While the grill is heating, spread butter over each side of the hamburger buns.

4. Butterfly the shrimp and coat with Lex's Pasilla Salt.

5. Add the shrimp and buns to the grill. Make sure the buns are facedown and away from direct heat.

6. Grill until the shrimp are opaque and the buns have a crispy, golden face.

7. Remove the shrimp and buns from the grill and put them on a plate.

8. To build the burgers, arrange the bottoms of the buns on a plate. Cover the bottom of each bun with 2 tablespoons of Coconut Curry Sauce.

9. Arrange about 4 shrimp per burger.

10. On top of the shrimp, lay down three mango slices per burger.

11. Add a four-finger pinch of cilantro to each burger.

12. Add 2 more tablespoons of Coconut Curry Sauce to the top of each burger, cover with the bun top, and serve.

SWEDISH MEATBALL BURGER

My biological father is a Swede and a lover of the finest foods, who exercises his patriotism by eating Swedish meatballs at every opportunity. But in the patriarchal Mexico of the 1970s and 1980s, where he lived, it was not fashionable for a man to cook. This is what the wife and maids were for. This recipe was originally given to me by his wife and my beloved stepmother, Keñya, a Palestinian-Mexican painter, who specializes in making Swedish meatballs, among many other things. Making meatballs, as it turns out, is more complicated than just smushing meat into balls. Ground beef is dense and heavy, and even when it is combined with breadcrumbs, it is quite limited, texturally speaking. But add veal, pork, and ground beef together and you'll have the folks from Sweden sniffing around your kitchen for the recipe.

MAKES 4 TO 6 BURGERS

½ medium onion, finely chopped

1 tablespoon butter

½ cup panko or breadcrumbs

½ pound ground beef

¼ pound ground pork

¼ pound ground veal

2 beef bouillon cubes or 2 tablespoons Bovril® beef extract, divided use

1 egg

½ cup milk

¾ cup cream

1 tablespoon flour

Salt and pepper to taste

4 to 6 potato buns

⅓ cup lingonberry jelly

1. In a saucepan, caramelize the onions in butter until they are brown and sweet. Let the mixture cool.

2. Mix in the panko or breadcrumbs, all the meats, 1 of the 2 bouillon cubes (or 1 tablespoon Bovril meat extract), and the egg. Mix gently but well.

3. Shape the meat mixture into 4 to 6 patties.

4. In a saucepan, over low to medium heat, combine the milk, cream, and the second bouillon cube (or 1 tablespoon Bovril meat extract).

5. Mix in the flour, and add the salt and pepper. Cook the mixture until the flour taste is gone, about 5 minutes. Add more milk, if the gravy is too thick.

6. Grill the meat patties for 3 to 4 minutes on each side over medium heat until they are golden brown.

7. Toast the buns over indirect heat.

8. Starting from the bottom bun, add 2 tablespoons of gravy, then the patty. Spread about 1 tablespoon of lingonberry jelly on the patty. Add 2 tablespoons of gravy to the top half of the bun and serve as a burger.

BURGER WITH FIG COMPOTE

Ground pork is great. The next time you visit your butcher ask him or her to grind up a good mixture of tenderloin, bacon, shoulder, or a combination of those. Be sure to keep some fat in the mix for good flavor, just as you would for beef patties. I usually make pork patties thinner than beef patties, since I'm not looking for a pink center. In fact I want these pork burgers well done (above 145°F).

MAKES 4 BURGERS

Fig Compote (page 178)

Baby arugula

1 pound 80/20 ground pork

1 tablespoon maldon salt

4 fresh brioche buns

20 currants

8 mint leaves

1. Prepare the Fig Compote and clean the baby arugula in advance. Set aside.

2. Bring the grill to medium heat.

3. Shape the ground pork into thin patties, ½-inch thick, and pat them dry.

4. Sprinkle the patties with salt, and grill them immediately for 7 minutes on each side.

5. Serve the burgers on a toasted bun with a generous dollop of Fig Compote and some baby arugula leaves.

6. Garnish with currants and mint leaves if desired.

BOURGEOIS BURGER

Truffle salt is divine. There is no doubt about that. But just like the bacon cover-up that has saved the day for so many mediocre burgers, truffle salt has become something of a magic medicine. It can be a cop-out for sure, but guess what? I'm cool with that. In fact, I'm so good with it that I'm happy to keep a little jar of the stuff in the pantry, knowing full well that the ingredients are, simply, salt and a few tiny specs of some low-grade truffle. The real thing will cost you your left arm and needs to be used quickly before the flavor fades. The fake stuff, on the other hand, will last a lifetime! When I'm feeling indolent and can't get a good flavor going, voilà! Truffle salt is a game changer. And, as it turns out, bacon has got nothing on fake truffle salt when it comes to making a solid bourgeois burger!

▶ MAKES 4 BURGERS ◀

1 pound 80/20 grass fed beef

Pinch kosher salt (optional)

4 white buns

2 ounces butter

1 heirloom tomato

1 red onion

4 ounces provolone cheese, 4 slices

2 ounces tomato ketchup

Egg Yolk Aioli (page 157)

¼ teaspoon truffle salt

1. Fashion 4 equal-sized patties 1 inches thick and as perfectly round as your OCD demands. You can mix some regular kosher salt into the patties, but be mindful that you will be adding truffle salt at the end.

2. Depending on the buns you have, you may want to slice off excess bread so that both sides of the bun are not much thicker than the patty. Butter each side of the buns, and set the buns aside.

3. Slice tomatoes ¼-inch thick and onions ⅛-inch thick. Set the slices aside.

4. Bring the grill up to medium-high heat, leaving an indirect grilling space for the buns that is low heat.

5. Grill patties on one side for 3 to 5 minutes, then flip. Grill the patties for an additional 3 to 4 minutes.

6. The patties will be medium rare when blood begins to appear on the tops.

7. Add a slice of provolone cheese to each one. Remove the cheese-topped patties from the heat and cover them.

8. Add the buns, buttered side down, over indirect heat. Grill until the buns are crispy and golden.

9. Arrange the burgers. Working from the bottom up, on the lower bun, add raw onion and ketchup. Then add the cheese-topped patty. Sprinkle a little truffle salt over the cheese. Add the tomato. Spread some aioli on the top bun. Serve.

3

HOT DOGS & SAUSAGES

T hese types of meat are ergonomically perfect and contain all the potential in the world to be held to the highest gastronomical standards. I'm excited to see more and more options in the supermarkets, especially hot dogs and sausages that are made without nitrates and other chemicals, and smaller brands that aren't tied up in the feed lot industry. Like the burger renaissance of the past 10 years, I think hot dogs are on their way up. Sausages, meanwhile, have deep cultural roots throughout the world, but the process of making them from scratch has stunted their popularity among backyard grillers. I am a novice at sausage making. But what I have realized is, with 40 bucks for a grinder and a stuffing tube, a weekend to spare, and an intrepid spirit, you can make your own great sausages at home.

HOT DOGS

When I think of hot dogs, I invariably think of New York City dirty-water–dog carts stationed anyplace where there are tourists. I think of the famous Coney Island hot dog eating competition with Joey Chestnut crushing 70 of them in 10 minutes! I think of Yankees games, and I think of my very first barbecues, when I started to play with exotic flavors on this most unassuming of meats. And I remember the only time my father ever cooked for me. He grabbed three frozen hot dogs out of the freezer, placed them in a scorching-hot, cheap tin pan, burned the ever-living-shit out of them in two seconds, and served them to me, still frozen on the inside and said, "Sorry, I don't have any buns!"

These slimy, stiff, rubbery mystery concoctions occupy a warm place in our hearts. Does anyone know what's in them or how they're made? No! Does anyone care? Not in the slightest. Nowadays everyone has allergies, gluten issues, lactose intolerances, and germ phobias. But eating a hot dog? No issues at all! It's incredible. Does it have nitrates? Yes! Does it contain very questionable animal parts? Of course. Is it carcinogenic? Maybe. Though their culinary value may be low, their sentimental value is huge!

With even the most perfunctory preparation, hot dogs can be served up with any number of thoughtful toppings. In fact, I see them as a vessel for vibrant and colorful salsas, pickles, chimichurris, and chutneys. With a growing number of natural versions on the market, hot dogs, I like to think, are growing up and ready for the big leagues.

CHIMICHURRI HOT DOG

The chimichurri hot dog changed the game for me, as far as grilling goes, as well as my general philosophy about food. Combining two seemingly disjoined elements—the familiar, unprepossessing hot dog with the unexpected fire of habaneros and cubanelles and a couple of other seemingly unlikely ingredients—really got me thinking for the first time about food. What exactly was it in the chimichurri and the hot dog that made them work so well together? And why is this combo not a "thing"? Well as it turns out, these two questions have become my mantra, and they have formed the first line drawn in a very large connect-the-dots game that has made me look at food, not as the end product of empirical recipes, but as a million dots that, potentially, can be connected in a million ways.

> ▸ MAKES 8 DOGS ◂

1 cup Chimichurri Sauce (page 154)

8 hot dogs

8 white hot dog buns

1. Prepare the Chimichurri Sauce in advance and set it aside.

2. Bring the grill to low heat. Lay the hot dogs perpendicular to the grates. This will keep them from falling between the grates when it is time to turn them.

3. Keep the buns closed, and place them over indirect heat. The grill should be covered while the buns grill. Remove the buns from the heat when they are crisp and golden.

4. Once the hot dogs are thoroughly warmed, paint them with a little oil and place them over high heat, keeping an eye on them so they don't burn.

5. When the skin is blistered but not charred, the hot dogs are done.

6. Serve the hot dogs on the warm buns with a generous dollop of Chimichurri Sauce on top.

BANH MI HOT DOG

Hot dog buns are the perfect vessel to which all kinds of vegetables cut lengthwise can be added. I find that some of these cut veggies also pair very nicely with hot dogs. The vegetables provide crunchy, crisp, sweet, and cool elements that are traditionally owned by ketchup and relish on a dog. Inspired by relish, I have taken to pickling everything that might be a worthy substitute. I've found that cutting various vegetables lengthwise and giving them a quick pickle works well on a dog. Add a little creamy component and this combo will appeal to purists and adventurers alike.

MAKES 8 HOT DOGS

Quick Pickling Brine (page 164)

Quick Pickled Vegetables (page 186)

Cucumber Aioli (page 155)

8 hot dogs

8 hot dog buns

1. Prepare the Pickling Brine and Pickled Vegetables at least 24 hours in advance.

2. Prepare and chill the Cucumber Aioli prior to starting to grill.

3. Bring the Pickled Vegetables and Cucumber Aioli to room temperature when you are ready to cook the hot dogs.

4. Bring the grill to a medium heat.

5. Grill the hot dogs perpendicular to the grill grates to create some grill marks and facilitate rolling.

6. Grill for 10 minutes while rolling $\frac{1}{4}$ turn every few minutes.

7. Remove the hot dogs from the heat. Place them in the buns, top with the Pickled Vegetables and Cucumber Aioli, and serve.

SWEET DUCK DOGS

I love a dirty-water hot dog from a street vendor in New York City. I always ask for a double line of ketchup, a single line of mustard, and a dollop of relish, if I'm feeling brash. The bun absorbs the moisture from the wet dog and the condiments, and it molds itself around the hot dog, which can then be eaten in two bites. I can easily slay ten of them at once. However, I always stop when I consider that $25 could also buy a nice sushi lunch. Therefore, the NYC street hot dog will forever be relegated to the snack category, at least for me. Here I've taken this cheap classic and given it some fancy rims and a paint job.

In this hot dog recipe, I've added duck fat. Whenever I grill duck, I always trim off as much of the fat as I can, for use later—for example, in this decadent recipe.

MAKES 8 HOT DOGS

2 cups trimmed duck fat, divided use

8 hot dogs

8 hot dog buns

½ cup sugar or honey

Coarse sea salt

4 to 5 scallions, chopped finely

1. Bring the grill to low heat.

2. In a saucepan, over a low temperature, heat the duck fat until it clarifies. This can be done on the grill; however, take extreme care not to let the grill get too hot, or the fat will burn. Once the duck fat is liquefied, reserve a couple of tablespoons to be used on the buns.

3. Simmer the hot dogs in the remaining fat for 5 minutes, stirring and rotating the dogs frequently to cover them with the fat.

4. Splay the buns and toast the insides for a minute or two over low heat on the grill. You want to get the inside of the bun crunchy.

5. Remove the hot dogs from the simmering duck fat, and either sprinkle them with sugar or spread a little honey over them.

6. Grill the hot dogs directly over medium-low heat for 10 minutes until the sugars begin to caramelize.

7. Meanwhile, remove the buns from the grill, and paint some of the reserved duck fat on the crunchy inside of the bun. Sprinkle them with coarse sea salt.

8. Add the hot dogs to the buns, and sprinkle chopped scallions over the top.

BACON DAWG!

What does a hot dog actually taste like? I mean, really? I think people eat hot dogs because of their texture, not their taste. Maybe this is why we have given them free reign to be stuffed into a bun and topped with anything at all. It doesn't matter what the topping is, as long as the dog has that familiar and tender snap when it's bent too far and has just the right amount of give when chomped on. Hot dogs are not too tough or chewy either, and, as all well know, they are great when paired with bacon.

> MAKES 8 HOT DOGS

8 hot dogs

1 pound bacon

8 hot dog buns

1 white onion, diced

2 Roma (plum) tomatoes, finely diced

4 to 5 scallions, chopped finely

Pinch of coarse salt

½ cup mayonnaise

1. Bring the grill to low heat.

2. Grill the hot dogs for about 10 minutes, rotating them often. For this recipe I prefer a hot dog that is not overly cooked, just heated up.

3. Grill the bacon until it is crispy. Wrapping bacon strips around tongs or skewers allows the bacon to be easily moved around on the grill, if there's a flare-up.

4. Splay the hot dog buns, and toast the interiors for a minute or two over low heat. You want to get the inside of the buns nicely toasted.

5. Mix together the onion, tomatoes, and scallions, and add a pinch of coarse salt.

6. Chop the grilled bacon strips into crunchy bits, and blend them into the vegetable mix at the last minute. (This will keep the bacon crispy.)

7. Pop a hot dog into each of the buns, dress it with the vegetable/bacon mix, and serve with a dollop (about 1 tablespoon) of mayonnaise.

SAUSAGES

Zoe walks up to me. She is five. On her face, she has that expression of a kid who has spent the last hour without any supervision and has gone deep into a lawless creative zone. She holds a dangling string of Play-Doh® that she ran through a toy sausage press (a gift from last Christmas). It's all tangled up with bits of Lego® and sparkles, and it looks like an elaborate hair scrunchie. "Daddy do you like my necklace?," she asks. My response is exactly the same as my wife Gladys's when, with more than a little dread, I show her my latest and greatest sausage endeavor and she comfortingly replies, "Ahhhh, I love it baby!"

I don't care what anyone thinks. Making sausage is fun! When we make them at home, as a family, it's the best time ever. It's a total mess, where unfiltered creativity can be ground up, stuffed, and enjoyed!

Like many of life's great accomplishments—shoelace tying, child rearing, PhD's, or completing a very large puzzle—once it's over it's just like, "Eh, that wasn't so bad." First of all, if you do not own a meat grinder, I will kindly ask that you get one this second. They only cost about 20 bucks; they are statuesque and will let all your guests know that you clearly know more than they do. Perception is everything. Second, find casings. This can potentially be the most difficult part of the whole process, since most supermarkets don't carry them—another good reason to shop from a butcher, who will have them on hand. Then, all you have to do is acquire some meat, garlic, and anything else lying around and throw it, and the grinder, into the refrigerator or freezer to get cold. Everything should be very cold in order for the grinder to work its magic. Then just grind, stuff, grill, and bask in your own glory. See? Easier than pie.

BACON SAUSAGES WITH MAPLE SYRUP

When you wake up at the crack of noon, you are faced with very serious dilemma: is it breakfast or is it lunchtime? Makin' bacon sausages filled with maple syrup and maybe a side of biscuits will solve this culinary dilemma.

> **MAKES 4 SAUSAGES**

1 pound bacon

1 pound pork shoulder

1 cup maple syrup

½ cup blueberries (optional)

1 tablespoon kosher salt

3-foot sausage casings (29-to-32-millimeter all-natural hog casings—ask your butcher for these)

3-inch butcher's twine

Pickles (optional)

EQUIPMENT

Manual meat grinder with sausage stuffer attachment

Wooden spoon

3-inch butcher's twine

Skewer, knife, or pin (ideal) with a sharp point

1. Cut the raw bacon and pork shoulder into 1-inch chunks.

2. Put the chopped bacon, pork shoulder, maple syrup, blueberries (optional), and salt into a freezer-safe bowl, and mix to combine.

3. Place the mixture in the freezer for 1 hour until it is very cold and stiff but not frozen solid. Also place the grinder in the freezer.

4. After 1 hour, remove the meat mixture and grinder from the freezer.

5. Attach the stuffing tube to the grinder, and carefully attach a casing to the stuffing tube. Tie off the end of the casing with a piece of butcher's twine.

6. Grind the mixture. Use a wooden spoon handle to help press the mixture into the grinder.

7. When the meat is fully ground, stuff the casing, adding a bit at a time.

8. With a skewer, knife, or pin (ideal) with a sharp point, prick out any trapped air.

9. Every 6 inches or so, twist the sausage casing.

10. Cut the casing in the middle of each twisted section.

11. Tie off the ends of the sausages with butcher's twine.

12. Bring the grill to medium-low heat.

13. Grill the sausages for 20 minutes, rotating them often until they are golden brown.

14. Serve the sausages in fresh buns with pickles and other appropriate fixins'.

WHITE HOTS

Go far enough upstate in New York, and you will surely encounter White Hots. These sausages were first introduced to Rochester by the German community back in the day. Anyone who has been to Europe knows that Germans make killer sausages with an order and sternness that commands respect. The Germans also know the merits of good mustards, which they use often and without remorse.

> MAKES 4 SAUSAGES

2 pounds bacon

2 pounds veal

½ cup yellow mustard

¼ cup whole grain mustard

¼ cup crushed red peppercorns

3 tablespoons white sugar

2 tablespoons horseradish (ground)

2 tablespoons Kosher salt

EQUIPMENT

Manual meat grinder with sausage stuffer attachment

Wooden spoon

3-inch butcher's twine

Skewer, knife, or pin with sharp point

1. Cut the veal, pork tenderloin, and bacon into 1-inch cubes. Freeze for 1 hour.

2. Mince the garlic, mustard, and habanero, and mix with the mustard and onion.

3. Remove the meat grinder and the meat from the freezer and combine with the onion, garlic, mustard, habanero pepper, and onion mixture.

4. Attach stuffing tube and casings. Tie off the very end of the casing with butcher's twine.

5. Add the meat to the grinder by hand, a bit at a time, and grind, making sure to keep feeding the grinder. Use a wooden spoon handle to keep the meat fed into the grinder.

6. Keep grinding all the meat to make a single, long sausage. Use a pin to prick the casing, and gently squeeze to remove any air pockets.

7. Once all meat has been stuffed, tie off the end with a 3-inch piece butcher's twine.

8. To make knots, find the middle of the long sausage by bending it in half so both ends touch. Twist once.

9. Decide the length of your sausages. Grab both ropes of sausage, overlap them, pinch them together, and twist twice.

10. Holding it up in the air with the two long ends dangling down, grab one long end and feed it through the hole you made and pull down to make a knot.

11. Continue until you have linked up all the sausage you made.

12. Grill over medium heat for 20 minutes, rotating often.

14. Serve in fresh buns with pickles and other fixins'.

BEEF RIB & MARROW SAUSAGES

Smoked bone marrow, spread generously over some Texas toast and topped with caramelized onions, parsley, and salt, is truly a thing of beauty. It's also a great thing to stuff into sausages!

> MAKES 4 SAUSAGES

4 to 6 marrow bones, 4 inches long (ask your butcher to halve these)

1 large red onion, thinly sliced

4 tablespoons butter

8 slices white bread, toasted until very dry

1 pound boneless beef rib

3 feet of sausage casing (approximate) to make 4 sausages 6 inches long

8 hot dog buns

1 cup fresh parsley, chopped

1 tablespoon coarse sea salt

EQUIPMENT

Manual meat grinder with sausage stuffer attachment

Butcher's twine, about 6 inches

Wooden spoon

Skewer, knife, or pin (ideal) with a sharp point

1. Place the marrow bones in a cast iron pot or in a tinfoil dish, and smoke them at medium-high heat for about 25 minutes. If you overdo it and the marrow runs, that's okay. Just make sure it doesn't burn in the bottom of the pan. Collect the marrow in a small cup or bowl. With a small spoon, dig around in the bones to collect any marrow that didn't melt down. Set aside until ready for use.

2. Caramelize the onions with butter over low heat for 30 minutes, stirring constantly. Set aside.

3. Toast the bread until it's dry and crispy, and then gently crush it into small crumbs.

4. Cut the beef rib into 1-inch cubes.

5. Combine the beef cubes, breadcrumbs, and smoked marrow until thoroughly mixed. Chill the mixture in the freezer for 1 hour. Place the grinder in the freezer as well.

6. After 1 hour, remove the meat mixture and the grinder from the freezer.

7. Attach the stuffing tube to the grinder and carefully attach a casing to the stuffing tube. Tie off the end of the casing with a piece of cooking string.

8. Grind the mixture. Use a wooden spoon handle to help press the mixture into the grinder.

9. Keep grinding all the meat to make a single, long sausage. Use a pin to prick the casing, and gently squeeze to remove any air pockets.

10. Once all meat has been stuffed, tie off the end with a 3-inch piece butcher's twine.

11. To make knots, find the middle of the long sausage by bending it in half so both ends touch. Twist once.

12. Decide the length of your sausages. Grab both ropes of sausage, overlap them, pinch them together, and twist twice. The technique is not unlike making balloon animals.

13. Holding it up in the air with the two long ends dangling down, grab one long end and feed it through the hole you made and pull down to make a knot.

14. Continue until you have linked up all the sausage you made.

15. Grill over medium heat for 20 minutes, rotating often.

16. Serve in fresh buns with pickles and other fixins'.

CHICKEN SKIN SAUSAGES WITH GRAVY AND BUTTERMILK BISCUITS

For this recipe, I get the fat content I want for the sausage from the chicken skin, which I finely chop before grinding. Chicken sausages are a great way to get major flavors. The entire reason for their being is just to supply a vessel for marinades, sauces, and rubs. Marinate the chicken, dry rub the skin, grind the meat, add flavored salt, pack it into casings, grill the sausages, and add gravy. Serve the sausages with some Grilled Buttermilk Biscuits. It's all but guaranteed to make your day brighter.

MAKES 4 SAUSAGES

Chicken Sausage Gravy (page 152)

Grilled Buttermilk Biscuits (page 179)

4 skin-on chicken legs

1/3 cup red onion, finely chopped

1/2 cup finely sliced leek

3-foot natural sausage casings

2 tablespoons coarse black pepper

1 tablespoon kosher salt

EQUIPMENT

Sharp kitchen knife

Manual meat grinder with sausage stuffer attachment

Cooking string

Wooden spoon

Butcher's twine

1. Prepare the Chicken Sausage Gravy and Buttermilk Biscuits ahead of time. Set aside and keep them warm until they are ready to serve.

2. Remove the skin from the chicken legs using a sharp knife and a paper towel to help you maintain a grip.

3. Cut the skin into small pieces about half the size of a postage stamp.

4. With a sharp kitchen knife, remove the meat from the bones. Cut the meat into 1-inch chunks.

5. Place the chopped chicken skin, the cubed leg meat, and the grinder into the freezer for 1 hour.

6. After 1 hour, remove the skin, meat, and grinder from the freezer.

7. Thoroughly combine the chilled skin, meat, onions, and leek in a bowl.

8. Attach the stuffing tube to the grinder, and carefully attach a casing to the stuffing tube. Tie off the end with a piece of cooking string.

9. Grind the chicken mixture. Use the handle of a wooden spoon to help press the meat into the grinder.

10. When the meat is fully ground, stuff the casing, adding a bit at a time.

11. With a sharp skewer, knife, or pin (ideal), prick out any air trapped in the casings.

12. Every 6 inches or so, twist the sausage casing.

13. Cut the casing in the middle of each twisted section.

14. Tie off the ends of the sausages with butcher's twine.

15. Bring the grill to medium heat.

16. Grill the sausages over the heat for about 30 minutes, turning them often.

17. Serve the sausages with the Chicken Sausage Gravy and Grilled Buttermilk Biscuits.

4

BEEF, PORK & LAMB

I've eaten at Peter Luger nine times, and I can recall each occasion in all its heavenly glory. Where the rest of life in New York can be a blur, stepping into this landmark demands your attention—and your respect. The décor is from a time before people cared about trying to exude an aura of old-worldliness like, say, every hipster spot surrounding it. It's just real. My grandfather used to be a member at Luger back in the day, when there was still sawdust on the floors. Today it's still a cash-only spot, and a man with a monocle sits in the corner of the restaurant counting, quite literally, huge stacks of cash.

The waiters are older men in bowties and aprons who, like most old-school Brooklynites, talk like movie characters and are annoyed to have to give you a menu. After all, what *exactly* did you come here for? The only consideration is how many people are eating (quite obvious) and who prefers beer or wine. These waiters are not tattooed hipsters making ends meet until their single-origin coffee stand selling out of a Volkswagen minibus takes off. These guys are in it for life. Most of them have worked at Luger so long they can do the job in their sleep, and they move about with complete control and confidence.

Though Luger is very secretive about how they make their steaks taste so good, I've eaten there enough to figure out the gist of it. And, what's shocking is that there really is no secret. First (which is always the first rule), they choose top-quality beef— that is, not from a feedlot. Second, they dry age the steaks for at least 42 days, which is standard. The enzymes break down the fibers in the meat, making it substantially more tender. Third, they dry the outside of the steak until it is bone-dry before cooking it. This helps give the meat a crispy crust. You can more or less duplicate this effect at home by covering your steak with cornstarch and salt and putting it in the freezer for 30 minutes before cooking. This treatment keeps the surface of the steak dry and cold and prepares it to take a blazing. I'm not sure exactly what Peter Luger does, but the process has got to be similar. And the final step? Cook that meat as if your life depended on it!

BEEF

Tenderloin, strip, ribeye, top sirloin, bottom sirloin (cheaper) blade, flank, flat iron (top blade), hangar (1 per animal), skirt (from plate section), T-bone, top round (London broil), tri-tip, brisket, chuck, short ribs, and ground beef.

GRILLING STEAKS

Nothing evokes more pride and fear in a grill master than a steak. To my mind, there is nothing more elemental to cook—nothing more visually primal and nothing quite as delicious. It's a rite of passage for all grillers. Grilling a perfectly thick, dry-aged steak with just fire, iron, and your instincts evokes (in me, at least) a great sense of accomplishment. Nothing will leave your guests more impressed and inspired than a juicy steak with a crispy crust.

I'll be honest, I avoided the big fancy steaks for a long time. A 2-inch-thick, dry-aged porterhouse or ribeye can cost up to $80 a pop at the local butcher, and carelessly overcooking it while debating what the crappiest or cheapest beers are with your friends would be a travesty. My take on it is that grilling with other folks nearby is fun and relaxing, and it's okay if sometimes a chicken wing falls through the grates. But when it's time for the big steaks, there can be no distractions and no mistakes. People can still talk to me when I'm grilling, but I will have already switched my social mode to autopilot: "Yeah? Cool! Okay . . ." My heart races when my inner clock calls time and I move the steak to a board to let it rest. It's a bold step that must be made with conviction and certainty. I've done the walk of shame back to the grill with a "not quite there" cut of meat, and I'm telling you . . . never again!

Steaks cook quickly and require focus and specific temperatures and cooking times. For example, a ¾-inch T-bone, one of the thinner steaks, needs very high heat to get a good crust in the short time it takes to cook to pink. A thicker Porterhouse requires more time to cook to pink and therefore a lower-temperature fire—or a very high-intensity fire for the crust, and then a move to an indirect heat source for 10 minutes. I recommend this method for 1¾-inch and larger steaks.

THE PORTERHOUSE

The king of steaks, the Porterhouse is a T-bone from the back end of the tenderloin. It contains the super-tender filet steak on one side and the flavorful New York strip on the other. There are also several nooks and crannies within the bones that hold some of the marvels of the cosmos. I like mine at 1 ¾ inches thick, so I can build up a super-thick crust while still getting a pink center. The thicker the steak, the more important it is to have it dry aged. During this process, enzymes within the meat will break down muscle tissue, which increases the tenderness. The results become very clear with thicker cuts.

SERVES 2

1 Porterhouse steak, 1¾ inches thick, approximately 1½ to 2 pounds

¼ cup cornstarch

¼ cup coarse salt

2 tablespoons coarse ground black pepper (optional)

1. Bring the steak to room temperature.

2. Pat the meat dry with a towel.

3. Mix the cornstarch and salt together until well blended.

4. Cover the steak on each side with the starch/salt mixture. Shake off any excess. Add some cracked pepper, if desired.

5. Place the meat in the freezer for 30 minutes.

6. Bring the grill to high heat. Then grill the steak over the heat for 5 to 6 minutes per side until a dark, hard crust forms.

7. If the steak is 1 inch thick, remove it from the heat at this time and let rest. If it is thicker than 1 inch, move it to hot, indirect heat and cook it for 5 minutes more for each ½ inch of thickness.

6. When the steak is done, remove it from the heat and let it rest for 5 minutes before serving.

FIRE AND FIRE TEMPERATURE

Fire is literally the best thing to ever happen to meat. It tenderizes the inside, creates crust, caramelizes the outside, breaks down proteins, renders fat, adds complex flavors, and kills any bacteria. Each and every cut of steak has its optimal fire temperature and time exposure. The key is to cook the steak exactly long enough to make a beautiful crust on the outside and have it at the preferred doneness inside. With too much heat the outside will burn before the inside reaches temperature, and vice versa. To add complexity, different cuts of meat change, based on how much that particular muscle was used. Cuts along the rump, chest, and neck tend to be tougher (and cheaper) and require low and slow cooking with indirect heat. Fatty, tender cuts around the lower back, ribs, and belly don't require much tenderizing and are perfect for grilling.

WAGYU TOMAHAWK RIBEYE STEAK (BONE-IN)

These are hands down the prettiest steaks in existence. Cuts weigh in around 2 pounds apiece and are about 2 inches thick. The ribeye is really one of the most flavorful cuts, and when you add in a Wagyu cattle breed and some dry aging, there is simply nothing better. These cuts, however, are expensive (some butchers sell them for 100 bucks a pop), so there is little room for error.

SERVES 2

1 (2-pound) Wagyu tomahawk ribeye steak (bone-in)

¼ cup cornstarch

¼ cup coarse salt

Cracked pepper to taste (optional)

1. Bring the steak to room temperature.

2. Pat the meat dry with a towel.

3. Mix the cornstarch and the salt until well blended.

4. Cover each side of the steak with the starch/salt mixture, and shake off any excess. Add cracked pepper, if desired.

5. Place the meat in the freezer for 20 minutes.

6. Bring the grill to high heat. Grill the steak over the heat for 5 to 6 minutes per side, until a dark, hard crust forms. If the steak is 1 inch thick, then remove it from the heat. If it is thicker than 1 inch, continue to cook the steak but move it to hot, indirect heat. Cook it for 5 minutes more for each additional ½ inch of thickness over 1 inch.

7. When the steak is done, remove it from the heat and let it sit for a few minutes before serving.

WHAT TO DO WITH THE FATS?

Trimmed fats should be placed in a small cast iron skillet and cooked alongside your steak at low temperature. When you're ready to serve the steak, add some butter to the skillet, along with a tiny squeeze of lemon or a pinch of rosemary. After the steak has rested for a few minutes, pour the fat/butter mixture over it right before serving, or pour it into a ramekin to serve alongside the steak. Adding sauce to the meat too soon will soften the hard-earned crust.

BLADE STEAK WITH CHILE DE ARBOL SALSA

Blade steaks are heavy on flavor, but not on cost. The reason for this is that blade steaks are chewy. There are two ways to avoid excess chewiness: You can cook blade steaks slowly, either by indirect heat or braised in a skillet. Or you can slice them thinly and sear them quickly on the grill. This recipe calls for the blade steak to be cubed and grilled slowly over low heat.

SERVES 4

1 cup Chile de Arbol Salsa (page 153)

4 blade steaks, ½ inch thick, approximately 1 pound

½ pineapple, peeled and hollowed out into a bowl

½ cup, red onion, diced

1 radish, sliced thin

¾ cup cilantro leaves, divided

1. Prepare the Chile de Arbol Salsa in advance. Set it aside until ready to use, but keep it hot.

2. Then bring the grill to low heat and cut the 4 steaks into 1½-inch cubes.

3. When the grill is ready, grill the steak cubes for 30 minutes.

4. After 20 minutes, add the pineapple bowl and gently grill upside down for 10 minutes. Then remove the pineapple from the grill, being very careful, as the grilled pineapple will become delicate.

5. When the meat cubes are ready, remove them from the heat. Toss the meat with onion, radish, and a little more than ½ cup of cilantro. (Set aside the remaining cilantro to be used for garnish.) Then place them in the grilled pineapple bowl.

6. Pour the Chile de Arbol Salsa over the top and garnish with the remaining cilantro.

ALWAYS LET A STEAK REST FOR A FEW MINUTES AFTER IT HAS BEEN REMOVED FROM THE HEAT. YOU CAN ROLL IT IN A BABY BLANKET OR JUST SET IT ON A COLD STUMP, DEPENDING ON YOUR MATERNAL INSTINCTS.

SKIRT STEAK

Skirt steaks always have a place on the table anytime I grill. They are relatively inexpensive, easy to cook, and super-flavorful. Unlike with a $100 ribeye, it is not blasphemous to load it up with all kinds of crazy rubs or sauces to shape its identity. I like to grill up a few skirt steaks right off the bat, when the coals are piping hot, and then serve it in little slices on a cutting board, with a bowl of Chimichurri Sauce alongside, for people to nibble on.

> SERVES 4 PEOPLE

Chimichurri Sauce (see recipe on page 154)

1-pound skirt steak

1 tablespoon coarse sea salt

1. Prepare the Chimichurri Sauce in advance, and set it aside until ready to serve.

2. Bring the steak to room temperature.

3. Pour burning coals from the chimney into a pile on one side of the grill. Spread out the coals for even distribution of heat under the grates. Bring the grill to high heat.

4. Pat the steak dry on both sides, and massage it with a generous amount of coarse sea salt.

5. Place the steak over direct heat, and grill for 3 minutes on each side. Then move it to a cutting board to sit for 3 minutes before serving.

6. To serve, cut the meat against the grain, at an angle. Serve is right on the cutting board with a bowl of Chimichurri Sauce for dipping.

ONE BENEFIT TO SLICING STEAKS THINLY IS THE AMOUNT OF SURFACE THAT CAN BE EXPOSED TO DRY RUBS AND SAUCES. THESE CAN TURN TOUGH, LESS-FLAVORFUL CUTS INTO SIZZLING LITTLE MORSELS.

TRI-TIP STEAK

Tri-tips are a big deal on the West Coast. They can be found everywhere and are served in every way imaginable. They're big, beefy, and tender when grilled just right. They also lend themselves well to brining, although they do not require it by any means.

SERVES 2 TO 4

Umami Brine (page 168)
1 (2- to 3-pound) tri-tip steak

1. Prepare the Umami Brine 2 days in advance. Add steak to 6 cups of the brine in a sealable container and refrigerate for 2 days.

2. After 2 days, remove the steak from the brine and bring up to room temperature.

3. Bring the grill up to medium heat.

4. Pat the steak dry and place it on direct heat.

5. Grill each side for 10 minutes. Then move the steak to indirect heat and grill for another 5 minutes on each side.

6. Let the steak sit for a few minutes before serving.

GRILL MARKS

We've all seen the commercials for some steakhouses, featuring the gray "steak meal" served with a side of "steamed vegetables" and maybe some "gravy" for something like $8.99. The philosophy of these places is that they can serve you pink slime, but as long as it has perfectly crisscrossed grill marks, then it's a bona fide steak! Nice try. It's all show and no go! If grill marks are a natural by-product of perfect execution, then all well and good, but they are not a requirement for perfect grilling. In fact, the grill marks only come when your grill has thick, heat-conducing grates that are themselves hotter than the fire below. With a blazing fire, all grill marks may be lost in the crust. This is a good thing. The whole steak is one giant grill mark. The thin grates on some grills simply cannot keep their heat when a big piece of meat is added and will not impart marks.

KOREAN BARBECUE RIBS

No matter where you are in New York City, Koreatown is just a few subway stops away, and no matter how old I get, dipping in and out of pool halls and karaoke joints on 32nd Street, it is always an invigorating place. Koreans know how to grill things better than just about anyone. Even after an epic feast, I'm lively and ready for ping-pong or a marathon. There is a balance in the food that respects good health and balance over everything. Grilled meats, fatty and succulent, are wrapped in lettuce and topped off with *kimchi* and other fermented *banchan* for digestion. Instead of encasing them in white bread buns, using lettuce makes even the most barbarous meat seem refreshing and clean.

SERVES 4

½ cup Quick Pickled Vegetables (page 186)

½ cup Lemonato Sauce (page 161)

2 (1-pound) flanken ribs, cut by the butcher to ⅛-inch thick

1 teaspoon fleur de sel (sea salt)

2 scallions

1 head butterhead lettuce

1. Prepare the Pickled Vegetables and Lemonato Sauce ahead of time. Bring them to room temperature before serving.

2. Bring the grill to high heat.

3. Chop the scallions and Pickled Vegetables, and clean the lettuce.

4. Pat the ribs dry, and massage them with fleur de sel.

5. Grill the ribs over high heat for 1 to 2 minutes on each side.

6. Treat the lettuce leaves as tortillas, and fill them with the sliced steak, Pickled Vegetables, scallions, and Lemonato Sauce.

BONELESS BEEF RIBS WITH CIPOLLINI ONIONS

Boneless beef ribs are perhaps the best steak for the money. Marbled with fat, they are tender and hugely flavorful. They are also much cheaper than a rib eye or porterhouse and are quite forgiving on the grill. I've been grilling these with caramelized cipollini onions for many years as a rustic gourmet dish.

> SERVES 4

8 to 10 cipollini onions

¼ cup olive oil

1 to 2 teaspoons coarse sea salt

2 to 3 boneless beef ribs, approximately 1 pound

½ teaspoon coarse black pepper

¼ cup honey or Whiskey Sauce (optional) (page 169)

1. Gently cut the small stems off the onions, and peel off the outer layer of the skin leaving the root intact to hold the onion together. Drizzle the onions with the olive oil and a pinch of salt. Set them aside.

2. Pat the boneless ribs dry, and massage them with the sea salt.

3. Bring the grill to medium high heat. Grill the steaks and onions over direct heat for 5 minutes on each side. Keep an eye on the onions. If they begin to get too dark, move them to a cooler side of the grill so they don't overcook.

4. Remove the boneless ribs from the heat, and let them rest on a platter for 5 minutes. During this time, attend to the onions to make sure they are soft, but not burned.

5. Remove the onions from the heat, and cut off the heel from each bulb. Chop the onions into quarters, and scatter them over the boneless ribs.

6. Serve with a drizzle of honey or Whiskey Sauce (page 169).

LAMB

The leg of lamb is a classic the world over, though it seems to take a back seat in American cooking. It's not standard fare for traditional American backyard barbecues, probably due to our obsession with burgers, dogs, steaks, and pork. In most Middle Eastern countries, the leg of lamb is happy to take the place of pork, which is not consumed there, and is offered up in a dizzying array of combinations. In fact, lamb adapts perfectly to the backyard grill or fire pit for a few good reasons: First of all, it's big and fun, which is a good place to start. Additionally, leg of lamb is very easy to cook; it serves a lot of people; and it has a rich, deep flavor that balances nicely with sweet sauces and light side dishes.

THE LAMB LEG FOOTBALL

The first way I like to do lamb is the football method, where you add some oil, salt, pepper, and herbs to the meat, wrap it several times in heavy-duty foil, and set it in the coals or build up the coals around the sides of the meat to roast it. Once the lamb is done, paint it with Honey Jalapeño Sauce, and grill it over direct heat to create a caramelized crust. Serve the lamb with more Honey Jalapeño Sauce on the side.

> SERVES 6–10

1 ½ cups Honey Jalapeño Sauce (page 159)

1 (3 to 4 pound) leg of lamb

½ cup olive oil

2 tablespoons salt

2 tablespoons course ground black pepper

4 cloves garlic

EQUIPMENT

Heavy-duty aluminum foil, about 3 feet long

Charcoal starter chimney

Charcoal briquettes

Wood chunks or wood sticks, as desired

Basting brush

1. Make the Honey Jalapeño Sauce in advance. Set it aside until ready to use.

2. Bring the lamb up to room temperature.

3. Peel and slice the garlic. With a small knife, make several incisions in the leg of lamb. Stuff the garlic slices into the incisions.

4. Unroll a 3-foot-long sheet of heavy-duty aluminum foil.

5. Place the lamb on the foil lengthwise.

6. Pour the olive oil over the lamb, and roll it around in the oil, coating it evenly.

7. Generously sprinkle the lamb with salt and pepper, making sure that it is evenly distributed over the meat.

8. Snugly wrap the lamb in at least two layers of foil, so that it is completely covered.

9. When you are ready to cook, fill a charcoal starter chimney with charcoal briquettes and get them burning well. Briquettes are best to use here, as they burn evenly and don't get as hot as lump coal.

10. Pour out the charcoal briquettes from the chimney, and arrange them into two lines along the bottom of the grill. Make each line of coals a little bit longer than the length of the rolled-up leg. Leave a few inches of space between the two lines where you'll place the leg. This is a better way to distribute the heat as opposed to just laying the meat on top of or next to the coals.

11. Bring the grill to a medium heat. Cook the lamb for 15 minutes in the coals. Then rotate the football by a half turn to expose the next side directly to the coals. Cook the lamb for another 15 minutes.

12. Continue this process, every 15 minutes, for 1 hour, and then remove the football from the coals.

13. Remove the leg of lamb from the foil, and arrange all the remaining coals in the grill into a single pile the length of the leg.

14. Position the grill grate over the coals and get it hot. Add wood chunks or sticks to impart desired wood flavor.

15. Divide the Honey Jalapeño Sauce and reserve half to serve with the meat. Use the remaining half of the sauce to paint all sides of the leg with a basting brush. Then place it over direct, medium-low heat. Rotate the leg slightly every 1 to 2 minutes, so the sugars caramelize but do not burn.

16. Once all the sides of the lamb are crispy, remove it from the grill. Let it rest for 5 minutes. Then slice and serve the meat with the reserved Honey Jalapeño Sauce.

LEG OF LAMB ON A SPIT OR CHAIN

When roasting a whole leg of lamb there is something to be said for seeing it roasting, not buried in the coals, but on a pedestal in all its glory, to be seen, appreciated for its sacrifice, and celebrated (and, later, munched on incessantly). Since lamb is so rich, perhaps it should not be heaped on a platter to be consumed all in one go. I prefer to roast it on a spit or suspended from a chain, rotating it often, and carving it as I go. This provides continuous small servings and keeps the hoards fed while other things go on and off the grill. This helps people avoid the mega food coma that comes from eating lots of lamb.

SERVES 6 TO 10

1 (3- to 4-pound) leg of lamb

10 cloves garlic

½ cup olive oil

2 tablespoons coarse rock salt

3 tablespoons course ground black pepper

1½ cups Honey Jalapeño Sauce (page 159)

EQUIPMENT

Small knife

Spit or chain

Aluminum foil

IF YOU PLAN TO HANG THE LAMB WITH A CHAIN, BE SURE TO KEEP ALL METALS AWAY FROM THE MEAT. AND NEVER USE GALVANIZED STEEL

1. Make the Honey Jalapeño Sauce in advance. Set it aside until ready to use.

2. Bring the lamb to room temperature.

3. Peel and cut each clove of garlic lengthwise into 4 slices.

4. With a small knife, stab multiple holes all around the lamb, ranging from 1 to 3 inches deep, and insert slivers of garlic into each.

5. Generously cover the lamb with oil, salt, and pepper.

6. Create a spit (see pages 13 to 15) or use a chain to hang the leg about 18 inches over the fire. Drill a hole in the bone and connect the chain at that point. Be sure to sweep any dust away and keep it away.

7. Arrange coals at the bottom of the pit (or grill). Then build a large wood fire in the pit (or grill) and let burn down to the coals. Ideally, you want a bed of coals much larger than the size of the lamb so the heat approaches the meat from many angles.

8. Grill over high heat for 1 hour, rotating every 10 minutes until all sides are crispy.

9. Wrap the leg of lamb in aluminum foil and place it on or near the coals. Cook for 45 minutes, but keep rotating the meeting and finding hot coals to lay it on.

10. Remove the aluminum foil and grill for another 15 minutes, rotating every 3 minutes.

11. Serve with Honey Jalapeño Sauce.

CARAMELIZED LAMB CHOPS

The hardest thing about grilling this sublimely decadent dish is the years of college, internships, and promotions one needs to put in before finally being able afford to buy the meat. But once you've got the dough, let the lamb chops rain down on everyone! They are juicy and rich and boast perfect little bone handles. They grill in 2 minutes on each side at high heat and require nothing for extra flavoring except some salt. But this is grilling, and we grillmeisters like to complicate things, to push the envelope, and we strive to attain otherworldliness. The only way I know how to do this is to take the sweet crunchy texture of crème brûlée and make it happen all around each lamb chop. It's so crazy it just might work!

> **SERVES 4**

¼ cup Simple Glaze (page 166)

8 lamb chops, 1 inch thick, approximately 1½ pounds

1 tablespoon salt

1 tablespoon black pepper

EQUIPMENT

Basting brush

1. Before cooking, prepare the Simple Glaze. Set it aside until ready for use.

2. Bring the chops to room temperature.

3. Pat the chops dry, and massage them with salt and pepper on both sides.

4. Bring the grill to medium-high heat. Then grill the chops over the heat for 2 minutes. Flip the chops and grill for 2 minutes more.

5. Before flipping the chops again, use a basting brush to paint a generous amount of Simple Glaze on each chop.

6. Flip the chops and grill them for 30 seconds. While they are grilling, paint the tops with the glaze. Once 30 seconds are up, flip the chops and repeat.

7. Each side should be grilled a total of 3 minutes.

PORK

Pork is perhaps the centerpiece—the hero of the archetypal American dinner: the Christmas ham, pork chops and applesauce, bacon and eggs. The glory of pork knows no bounds. Its flavors and dimensions are numerous and grandiose, from a slow-cooked shoulder and ribs to roasted chops and sizzling bacon, each cut is worthy of celebration and endless joy! Ranging from lean to fatty, tender to firm, pork is also very receptive to brines and sauces, allowing the meat to mingle with just about anything. Few things are as delicious as perfectly smoked baby back ribs or marinated chops, and few, if any foods, are as cherished and adored as bacon or as divine as a cured jowl.

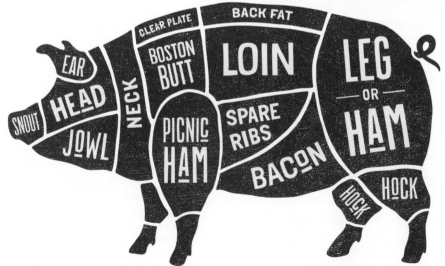

MOLASSES BRINED PORK CHOPS

Pork chops and brine are as close to molecular biology as I am likely to achieve in this lifetime. Because pork is lean, it lends itself well to brining. Though there is much debate about the possible advantages (if any) to brining, there are two facts: 1. Meat that is brined weighs more afterward, indicating that it has absorbed moisture. 2. Brining will most certainly add flavor to meat, regardless of whether the time or energy is warranted to achieve this.

SERVES 4

Molasses Brine (page 163)

4 bone-in pork chops, 1¼ inch thick, 2 pounds; preferably never frozen and of heritage breed

1. In advance, prepare the Molasses Brine, and brine the chops in the refrigerator for at least 1 day, but preferably for 3 days.

2. Remove the chops from the refrigerator, and bring them to room temperature.

3. Bring the grill to medium heat.

4. Pat the chops dry, and grill them for 5 to 6 minutes on each side.

5. Remove the chops from the grill, and let them rest for a few minutes before serving.

6. Serve with caramelized apples or freshly made applesauce.

DENATURATION

Denaturation is the process that breaks down protein fibers in meat with either heat, salt, acid, or a combination of the three, to make it tender. Even a tender ribeye needs to be exposed to heat and cooked in order to be chewable. Sometimes, long exposure to low heat is necessary to do the trick (as with brisket).

Dry-aging, brining, and acidic marinades all can tenderize meat, as well. Osmosis is the scientific process that explains the removal of moisture with salt. By salting a piece of meat and letting it sit, moisture will be drawn out of the meat, a process known as salt-curing. In the reverse operation of brining meat, meat is soaked in a salt brine, that is, salt dissolved in water., The brine is absorbed into the meat, which increases moisture content. When the brine is flavored with additional ingredients, it saturates the meat, which gets a whole lot of tastiness going.

RIBS & FIGS

Typically I like to smoke ribs in an offset smoker, but they do very well on the grill on low heat and with a little help from tinfoil to help retain moisture. Figs add a sweet and bold flavor that complements the smokiness of the ribs.

> SERVES 2 TO 3

1 cup Basic Barbecue Sauce (page 150)

1 cup Fig Compote (page 178)

1 rack baby back pork ribs (approximately 2 pounds)

Salt and pepper to taste

EQUIPMENT

Aluminum foil

Kitchen towel

PERFECTLY COOKED MEAT DOESN'T HAVE TO "FALL OFF THE BONE," BUT IT SHOULDN'T BE A CHORE TO CLEAN THE BONE, EITHER.

1. Prepare Basic Barbecue Sauce and Fig Compote in advance. Set aside.

2. Remove the shiny membrane from bone sides of the ribs by scoring across the last bone of each rib with a knife. With a paper towel, grab the membrane and peel it off.

3. Bring the grill to medium heat, with the coals arranged on one side, leaving enough room for the rack of ribs. Use wood chunks, wood chips, or sticks to enhance the flavor of the meat. With a good exposure to smoke, the meat will reveal a pink ring around the edges, called a *smoke ring*, when it is sliced.

4. Salt and pepper the ribs, and then lay the ribs on the grill meat side up.

5. Grill the ribs over direct heat for 30 minutes, flipping often.

6. Wrap the ribs in aluminum foil and cook on medium, indirect heat for 3 hours. Rotate the ribs every 30 minutes or so for even heat distribution.

7. Remove the ribs from the foil and paint them with barbecue sauce on both sides. Grill each side over direct heat for 15 minutes, flipping the ribs every 5 minutes. Keep the fire temperature low so they don't burn. When the meat starts to pull back along the edges, revealing the bone, it is done.

8. Remove the ribs from the grill, and let them rest, covered, for 10 minutes.

9. Serve with the Fig Compote.

UMAMI PORK CHOPS

Sometimes, in my quest to find the perfect recipe, I find an alternate variation that may not be *better* but is unique and powerful in its own right. Take, for example, the lowly pork chop, destined to be served up with some applesauce and boiled peas. My attitude changed when I had the Kurobuta pork chop at Momo Sushi Shack in Bushwick, Brooklyn; I realized that a simple chop can rise to another level. Luckily, Phil, the owner, is an old friend who offered me the recipe for this book. But, I figured, why stop my madness when it has taught me to cook? So I declined the official recipe, but accepted the information that the chop was brined for 3 days with, among other things, mushrooms and seaweed. This was enough for me to go on, and after several attempts, I think I've made something as worthy as Phil's creation that still has something in it that is distinctly mine.

SERVES 4

Umami Brine (page 168)
4 bone-in pork chops, 1¼ inches thick, preferably unfrozen and of heritage breed

1. Prepare the Umami Brine in advance. Soak the pork chops in the brine, refrigerated, for a least 1 day but preferably for 3 days.

2. Remove the meat from the refrigerator and from the brine, and bring it to room temperature.

3. Bring the grill to medium heat.

4. Pat the chops dry, and grill them for 5 to 6 minutes per side.

5. Remove the meat from the grill, and let it sit for a few minutes before serving.

PORK TENDERLOIN

Whenever I think of a pork tenderloin for dinner, it's always in the context of some family dinner with the boring side of the family. It's safe, easy, and lends itself well to herbs and simple sides. A pork tenderloin cooks in about 25 minutes, in just about any pot, and is big enough to serve a whole table of Weight Watchers®. It's also modestly celebratory and can easily be sliced and served (picture the server: a smiling 60-ish matriarch in a checkered apron). It could just be that I'm too far removed from the tenderloin game these days and ignorant of any "rad" renditions, but whenever I imagine the perfect tenderloin it's been burned, blackened, and doused with spice.

SERVES 4

Molasses Sauce (page 163)

1 (3-pound) pork tenderloin

1 tablespoon kosher salt

1 serrano pepper, finely chopped

Sprigs of cilantro

EQUIPMENT

Basting brush

1. Prepare the Molasses Sauce in advance. Set it aside.

2. Bring the grill to medium heat.

3. Pat the tenderloin dry, and massage it with salt.

4. Grill the tenderloin over medium heat, rotating it often, for 10 minutes.

5. Brush on the Molasses Sauce, and grill the meat for an additional 5 minutes, paying close attention so that the sugars do not burn. The tenderloin should have a very dark, caramelized crust.

6. Remove the tenderloin from the heat, and let it rest for 5 minutes. Add fresh, finely chopped serrano pepper, and garnish with sprigs of cilantro.

BACON STEAKS

Whenever I come across pork belly at the butcher I simply must buy it. Pork belly comes with a huge piece of skin, great for making chicharron chips, and it has lots and lots of bacon. In its entirety, bacon is easy to cook on the grill, and since it takes a while, it can really absorb good flavors from a wood fire. Scoring the skin before grilling is crucial, as it is along these score lines that the steak can later be cut (without them, the thick, crunchy skin can be hard to cut later with a knife). If you like, score cross hatches 1-inch apart, and after cooking, cut the steak into 1-inch cubes as appetizers, or serve them any size you like.

MAKES 4 STEAKS
OR ABOUT 40 CUBES FOR APPETIZERS

3-pound pork belly with skin on

2 tablespoons sea salt

2 tablespoons coarse black pepper

Water or apple juice

EQUIPMENT

Sharp knife

Spray bottle

Meat thermometer

1. Bring the pork belly steak up to room temperature.

2. Bring the grill up to high heat with coals and have some wood chips, chunks, or sticks on hand to add smoke later. Create an indirect grilling area large enough for the steak.

3. With a sharp knife, score the skin diagonally down the entire length of the pork belly steak. The cuts should be 1 inch apart. Make a separate set of score lines perpendicular to the first set of score lines.

4. Apply salt and pepper with your hands, massaging it into all the nooks and crannies.

5. Cook the steak, skin side down, over high heat for about 6 minutes until the skin starts to blister and makes cracking noises. If a flare-up occurs, spray the meat with water or apple juice, or move it away from the direct heat until the flames calm down.

6. Once the skin side is a golden brown with blisters, flip the meat and move it to indirect heat. Add some wood to the fire (away from the steak) and close the lid.

7. The pork belly should cook at indirect, medium-high heat for about 1 hour until it reaches an internal temperature of 160 degrees.

8. Remove the meat from the heat and cover. Let it rest for 5 minutes.

5

POULTRY

In 2005 I had the bright idea to do a road trip from Brooklyn to Mexico City. After all, what could possibly go wrong, what with the "narcos," corrupt "federales," and very dangerous highways, not to mention my own devices? One night after several generous servings of whiskey, I found myself stumbling about in front of St. Jude's church, the patron saint of lost causes in Williamsburg. There, in the glistening moonlight was an early 1990s Chevy conversion van for sale, complete with a boomerang antenna, creepy curtains, and wood trim. I grew up knowing these as "rapist mobiles." I woke up the next day at the crack of noon and returned to the wagon. Two Mexican guys owned it and used it to transport empty cans. Asked if it would make the 5,000 miles to Mexico City, the two guys looked at each other, then back at me, and slightly out of sync replied unconvincingly, "Sí." I was sold! A man will believe whatever he wants to believe. And I believed that this van, with just the right amount of rust and dentage would be the perfect camouflage for an epic, 6-month Mexican road trip. *Adelante, güey!*

Five months later, I'm in Tepoztlán, a small town in the mountains between Mexico City and Acapulco. I'm hanging out at a rotisserie chicken stand that looks like some sort of medieval torture device. It's a man-sized iron cage with heavy, iron gears on each side that turn a large shaft. From this shaft orbit smaller shafts, each fitted with cages locking in butterflied chickens. Near the back of the cage is a raging hardwood fire, so the rotating cages with splayed chickens are themselves passed through the fire. It's the best chicken I've ever had. EVER! I'm talking with the owner, Israel, trying to tease out some secrets. We make small talk. He tells me how he had a dream to get into the United States, and after years of trying, finally made it. But when he scored a job at a Boston Market in Maryland, he was basically like, "This sucks!— I'm going back!"

Israel's stand is right outside the outdoor market in Tepoztlán. School kids in pressed blue uniforms scuttle about drinking "juice" out of plastic bags. Little abuelitas hunch over their produce for the day. A three-legged dog hobbles by, as a young boy, maybe 4, swats at it with a tasseled toy wand. An old Ford F-150 pulls up. In the back a giant bull is tied up, its head strapped uncomfortably to the metal siding, just like one would tie down an ATV. A cowboy jumps out.

He's got the boots, big buckle, and a cowboy hat with a pin of a cowboy boot set right in the front. What a dude! He ducks in under the low-slung tarps and enters the market.

Here in the shadows, folks sell everything from pirated DVDs, slingshots, Dora the Explorer balloons, copal, masks, mugs, hammocks, ladders, to food—there are rows upon rows of food stands. Metal tables adorned with glorious clay bowls filled with meats, stuffing, and sauces encircle a central workspace with an inverted wok and a tortilla press where the doñas work their magic.

Rather than squinting up at the menu, you just lay your eyes on the bounty before you. Bowls of lengua, chorizo, longaniza, chicken, arrachera, salchicha, bistec, goat, and cecina. Dishes of flowers, cactus, crickets, chicharron, mushrooms, potatoes, tinga de pollo. And below them there are smaller bowls, filled with salsas. The best stands feature a dozen of them. Thick, sweet, refreshing, sour, smoky, spicy, or any variation of these tastes are made from watermelon, peanut butter, Coca-Cola, peaches, tamarind, ground crickets, pineapple, tomatoes, and hundreds of species of peppers, used either fresh, smoked, or dried. In turn these peppers can be fried, boiled, or lightly toasted, before use, to further enhance their effect.

Mexico has more types of chiles than anywhere else on Earth. While in the United States, we are quite accustomed to serrano, jalapeño, and canned chipotle, it's amazing that the other types haven't gained more popularity. With their complex balance of smokiness, sweetness, and spice, they make the absolute best bases for traditional American barbecue sauces.

I order a quesadilla with *chicharron prensado,* mixed with some *queso seco* and topped with crispy onion and a refreshing green sauce, made to order on a blue masa tortilla. I somewhat hope the *doña* will be impressed with my familiarity and creativity with her specific cuisine, but instead she just yells to the cook, "He wants a *tlacalo macho,*" or something to that effect, and goes back to texting.

Ok, so my invention already had a name and was apparently not original at all around here, but that's fine with me.

WHOLE GRILLED CHICKEN

A whole grilled chicken is a thing of beauty. It takes on great flavors from a smoky fire, goes well with just about any other food, and cooks in one hour without any tinkering or fuss.

> SERVES 4

Buttermilk Marinade (page 152)

1 whole chicken, preferably hormone free, humanely raised, about 2 pounds

2 tablespoons olive oil

1 teaspoon Maldon sea salt or kosher salt

1. Prepare the Buttermilk Marinade at least 1 day in advance.

2. Marinate the chicken in the Buttermilk Marinade overnight in the refrigerator.

3. Remove the chicken from the refrigerator, bring it to room temperature, and pat it dry. Discard the marinade.

4. Douse a paper towel with oil and rub it all over the chicken. Then add a salt or rub of your choosing. I love this with Lex's Pasilla Salt recipe or michelada salt.

5. Heat the grill to medium, arranging the coals to leave an open space for indirect grilling. Note that making a wood fire with hickory will yield the most amazing flavor.

6. Clean the grates of the grill, and position the chicken, breast side up, in a hot area, but not where the coals give off more than a medium-high heat (400° F).

7. Grill the chicken for a total of 60 to 75 minutes, depending on its size. **Keep the grill lid closed except when adding coals and rotating chicken.**

8. After 20 minutes on the grill, begin another chimney of coals. Also rotate the chicken 180 degrees, while keeping it breast side up.

9. Once the coals are going, about 15 minutes or so, open the grill, and gently pour in the fresh coals from the chimney so the chicken is still cooking with indirect heat. You will know that the coals are

ready when they are no longer black and are glowing orange. You can (read that as *should*) always add some wood chips or sticks for flavor at any point during the cooking.

10. The chicken should only be moved two or three times during the grilling and can easily be picked up with leather gloves or by inserting a wooden spoon in the cavity. Extreme care should be given not to tear the skin or puncture the flesh. Metal tongs are not advised.

11. Remove the chicken from the grill, and let it rest in a casserole dish or bowl to catch the juices before serving.

YOU CAN SERVE ROAST CHICKEN WITH JUST ABOUT ANYTHING. WHEN I ROAST A CHICKEN OVER A WOOD FIRE, I LIKE TO SERVE IT WITH FRESH GREEN SALSA (PAGE 158) OR CHIMICHURRI SAUCE (PAGE 154) AND A SIDE OF TENDER SLAW.

SKINLESS CHICKEN BREASTS WITH LEMONATO SAUCE

Sometimes our dreams of grilling a glistening whole hog are crushed by the reality that there are people, who, in fact, would prefer to eat a skinless chicken breast. We could chase away these domesticated divas with a flaming stick, but as the host and grill master who am I to deny my guests? After all, as far as meats go, skinless chicken is healthy, and with the right approach, it can be juicy and tasty, too.

SERVES 4

Green Michelada Salt (page 139)

Lemonato Sauce (page 161)

4 skinless chicken breasts, about 1½ pounds

¼ cup peanut oil

Salt and pepper to taste

4 oranges slices, about ⅛ inch thick (optional)

1. Prepare the Michelada Salt and Lemonato Sauce in advance. Set them aside until ready for use.

2. Rinse and bring the chicken breasts to room temperature and pat them dry.

3. Bring the grill to medium-high heat.

4. Douse a paper towel with the peanut oil and rub it all over the chicken breasts. Then add a salt or rub of your choosing. For this recipe I use a green Michelada Salt.

5. Place each piece of chicken over direct heat and, if you like, insert a ⅛-inch slice of orange under the thin side of each breast to reduce the heat and ensure even cooking.

6. Grill the chicken breasts over direct heat for 7 minutes on each side.

7. Remove the chicken from the grill. Let it rest for 2 minutes, and top with Lemonato Sauce.

CANDIED CHICKEN POPS

If someone were to approach me to make a movie about food, it would be a riff on *Jiro Dreams of Sushi*, and would be called *Lex's Dreams of Candied Meats!* It doesn't roll off the tongue so well, but who gives a shit. The sad, weird truth is that I do dream of candied meats. I do so for several reasons: (1) Sweet, crunchy, glazed meats are the greatest things to eat. (2) They pair nicely with fresh greens, such as butterhead lettuce, crispy Romaine, and the like. The balance between sweet and heavy, and meaty and light, and crispy and refreshing adds a crucial dynamic to any grill. I think vegetables are awesome to accompany a grill, especially when they're raw. (3) Sweet glazed meats are filling, and a little goes a long way. (4) They are hard to do right, which makes obsessing over them particularly rewarding.

SERVES 4 TO 5

Sweet Tare Glaze, divided (page 166)

10 chicken drumsticks, about 1½ pounds

2 tablespoons kosher salt

1 cup canola oil

Scallions for garnish (optional)

White sesame seeds for garnish (optional)

EQUIPMENT

Aluminum foil or a muffin pan

Basting brush

1 ramekin, for the dipping sauce

1. Prepare the Sweet Tare Glaze in advance. Divide into portions using ⅓ cup for grilling and reserving ⅔ cup to serve with the grilled chicken. Set aside.

2. Score the drumsticks directly above the round end-bone with a knife, in order to cut all skin and tendons.

3. Prop a drumstick against a table with the bone facing up, and use your fingers to push down the meat, revealing the bone.

4. Then tuck the meat on the drumstick inside the hole to resemble a lollipop.

5. Rub the meat with salt and canola oil.

6. Place each drumstick, meat end down, onto a 4×4-inch sheet of foil.

7. Wrap the meat end of each drumstick in foil, and shape it into a ball. Or braise the drumsticks in a muffin pan (see the box "Making the Chicken Pops in a Muffin Pan" on page 100).

8. Grill the foil-covered drumsticks over low heat for 20 minutes, turning them every 5 minutes or so.

9. Remove the foil, and thoroughly brush the drumsticks with the Sweet Tare Glaze.

10. Grill the drumsticks over medium heat, rotating them often, for a total of 5 minutes to caramelize the sugars.

11. Serve the drumsticks alongside a ramekin with reserved Sweet Tare Glaze for dipping.

MAKING THE CHICKEN POPS IN A MUFFIN PAN

As an alternative to wrapping chicken drumsticks in aluminum foil and grilling them, why not braise them in a muffin pan? Here's how to do that.

1. Coat the inside of the muffin pan with a generous amount of canola oil.

2. Salt the drumsticks if you haven't done so already.

3. Place a drumstick into each muffin hole with the bone sticking up.

4. With your hands, gently form the chicken inside the hole into an even shape. The chicken will take on this shape when cooking, so it's best to have it arranged well.

5. Place the muffin pan in the grill over indirect heat and cook the chicken for 45 minutes at medium-high heat.

6. Remove the pan and gently pull out each drumstick. Coat the drumsticks with tare sauce and serve.

DOUBLE-BAKED CHICKEN THIGHS

The double deep-fry is a classic Korean method for preparing chicken, the idea being that if a chicken wing needs to be deep-fried for 12 minutes, instead of doing it all in one go, fry it for 6 minutes, remove the chicken, let it cool, and then fry it again for another 6 minutes. This may sound like pseudoscience or hocus-pocus, but anything that requires deep-frying food that has already been deep-fried is an idea with legs, and I'm willing to run with it. On the grill, you can roast the meat, cool it, and then roast the roast again. Hey, you can roast the meat, cool it, and then deep-fry the inside of whatever you're grilling! You can also deep-fry the meat, paint it with sauce, and then finish it all on the grill. But the essence is to fry the fry, one way or another. Here I bake chicken legs, cool them until the skin hardens, and then bake the legs again. That creates extremely crispy skin.

SERVES 4

1 cup Honey Mustard Barbecue Sauce (page 160)

4 chicken legs (drumstick and thigh)

¼ cup cornstarch

Cilantro, a handful of fresh leaves for garnish

1. Prepare the Honey Mustard Barbecue Sauce in advance. Set it aside until ready for use.

2. Make a wood fire. Let the coals settle, but still keep it hot! Clear an area for indirect grilling. Have small wood sticks, chips, and chunks available to add to keep the grill hot.

3. Thoroughly and evenly apply dry rub to the chicken, either right before grilling or the day before, to absorb more flavor. Regardless, make sure the chicken is at room temperature before grilling.

4. Arrange the legs skin side up, away from the direct heat. Cook them for 15 minutes.

5. Flip and grill the chicken, skin side down, for 10 minutes with indirect heat. Remove the chicken from the grill, and add more wood to the grill to make sure it's hot for the next round.

6. Allow the chicken to cool for 10 minutes in the refrigerator.

7. Pat the chicken dry and apply a thin, even coating of cornstarch to all sides of the legs and thoroughly remove any excess.

8. Return the chicken to the grill, skin side up. Ideally, the temperature of the grill should reach 500°F, which is easily attainable if you have flames.

9. Roast the chicken for 15 minutes. Do not flip the chicken; instead, rotate it halfway through the process.

10. Remove the chicken. Let it rest for a few minutes. Serve with cilantro garnish.

CHICKEN YAKITORI

Whatever happened to kebabs—those hefty cubes of beef separated by chunks of onion and red pepper? Fixtures at every barbecue, the kebabs were invariably tough, overcooked, or undercooked. What they needed was discipline, a process, and an artful approach. Enter Japanese *yakitori*. These elegant croquettes are definitely the faster, stronger, smarter, and better-looking siblings of those extinct behemoths of barbecues past.

SERVES 8

1 cup Chimichurri Sauce (page 154), Basic Barbecue Sauce (page 150), or Lemonato Sauce (page 161)

2-pound chicken with skin on

3 to 4 ounces Gouda cheese

2 eggs

1 cup panko, divided

1 tablespoon salt

2 to 3 tablespoons olive oil for basting

1. Depending on which sauce you opt to use with this dish, prepare the Chimichurri Sauce, Barbecue Sauce, or Lemonato Sauce in advance.

2. Remove the meat from the bones and discard the bones. With a good knife, finely chop the dark and white meat of the chicken, as well as the chicken skin, into pea-sized pieces. Mix together thoroughly.

3. Cut the cheese into pea-sized pieces.

4. In a bowl, beat the eggs and mix in $1/2$ cup of the panko (reserve the other half). Add the salt. Mix well. Incorporate the cheese.

5. Gently and lightly, mix together 1 ounce of the egg mixture with 3 ounces of the diced chicken mixture to form an egg shape. Repeat until you have formed 8 croquettes.

6. Put the croquettes in the refrigerator for about 40 minutes to firm them up.

7. Bring the grill to medium heat.

8. Remove the croquettes from the refrigerator; paint them with olive oil; and then coat the croquettes with a thin layer of the reserved panko.

9. Oil the grill, add the croquettes, and grill them, rotating them often, for 15 to 20 minutes. Remove them from the heat, and let them cool for a few minutes.

10. Serve the croquettes with Chimichurri Sauce, Barbecue Sauce, or Lemonato Sauce.

RANCH CHICKEN

I've known ranch dressing my whole life. When I was a kid, it was served alongside celery and carrots. In college, we would dip our pizza into it, chicken wings too. Ranch is rich, creamy, and has that *je ne sais quoi* factor required of any popular American condiment. It seems the only thing ranch dressing is not very well suited to is salad. The flavor is strong, and the formula is so completely unhealthy that pairing it with some nice, organic mixed greens is unthinkable. But marinate your chicken in the stuff overnight and it makes an instant classic.

SERVES 4 PEOPLE

1 whole chicken

1 (16-ounce) bottle ranch dressing (any brand!)

2 tablespoons peanut oil

Salt or your choice of dry rub (see Lex's Pasilla Salt, page 141)

1. If you are intending to use Lex's Pasilla Salt for the dry rub, prepare it in advance. Set it aside until ready to use.

2. Rinse the chicken and pat it dry. Place the chicken in a resealable plastic bag, and pour in the ranch dressing to completely coat the chicken.

3. Press any trapped air out of the bag, seal it, and refrigerate it for at least 4 hours and up to 2 days.

4. When you are ready to grill, light a chimney filled with briquettes. When they are bright red, pour them into a pile on one side of the grill.

5. Remove the chicken from the bag and rinse off the dressing. Pat the chicken dry.

6. Cover the chicken lightly with oil and add your favorite salt or dry-rub mixture.

7. Grill chicken whole breast side down at medium-high heat for 1 hour to 1 hour and 15 minutes, depending on the weight of the chicken. Do not poke or prod the chicken while it is cooking. Halfway through the cooking process, rotate it (do not flip it over) 180 degrees to expose the other side to the heat.

8. When the chicken is a dark golden brown, remove it from the grill, let it rest for a few minutes, and then serve it.

MEXICAN BULGOGI DRUMSTICKS

These drumsticks conjure up memories of a sunny day with my family, kids scrambling around, and my friends and their kids all doing what people need and love to do: eating and being social. As the grill master, I love the responsibility of transforming inedible chunks of flesh into succulent gold and doling it out. I picture Bill Murray in *What About Bob?*, devouring Fay's chicken and moaning with delight. Few other experiences in life are this rewarding and awesome! This recipe is party favorite Numero Uno. It never fails. If Metallica's *Ride the Lightning* were a drumstick, this would be it.

> **SERVES 4 TO 8**

1 cup Mexican Bulgogi Marinade (page 162)
8 chicken drumsticks

1. Prepare the Mexican Bulgogi Marinade at least 1 day in advance, and refrigerate it until it is ready for use.

2. Prep the chicken at least 4 to 8 hours before you are ready to begin grilling. Rinse and pat the drumsticks dry. Place them in a resealable bag and pour the marinade into the bag.

3. Press any air out of the bag and seal it. Thoroughly massage the chicken to incorporate the marinade.

4. Marinate the chicken for 4 to 8 hours in the refrigerator. (Two hours of marinating imparts a slight hint of flavor, but 10 hours is too much.)

5. After 4 to 8 hours, remove the chicken from the refrigerator and bring it to room temperature.

6. Bring the grill to medium heat.

7. Grill the drumsticks for 30 minutes, rotating them often.

8. To serve, fold a napkin in half diagonally, and it wrap tightly around the base of each drumstick.

STUFFED HEN ON A STAKE

Grilling things on stakes is fun, but there are also some practical reasons for using this method. For one, the food never touches the grill. Hens are perfect for stakes because they are small, they cook relatively quickly, and the skin gets amazingly crunchy. You can also stuff them with anything you like.

SERVES 1

½ cup Heirloom Pico de Gallo (page 159)

1 Cornish hen, about ½ pound

1 baby zucchini, sliced thin

⅓ cup Brie cheese, thinly sliced

¼ cup prosciutto, roughly chopped

¼ cup olive oil

Salt and pepper to taste

EQUIPMENT

3 sturdy green sticks (not poison ivy!) to be used as stakes

1. Prepare the Heirloom Pico de Gallo in advance. Set it aside.

2. Bring the hen to room temperature, rinse it well inside and out, and pat it dry.

3. Make a wood fire, preferably with hickory, and let it burn down to coals.

4. Since hens are small, they can be cooked like marshmallows on a stick; although it's helpful to either prop up the stick with a rock or work it into a hole in the ground so that it can hang over the fire on its own.

5. Roast the hen for 30 minutes over medium-high heat until it is golden brown and crispy.

6. On a grate on a stone by the fire, cook the zucchini for about 15 minutes until soft. Rotate after 7 minutes for even heat distribution.

7. Remove the hen from its stake, and immediately stuff it with the zucchini, cheese, and prosciutto.

8. Let the hen rest for 5 minutes before serving it with the Heirloom Pico de Gallo.

WHOLE DUCK WITH HONEY AND CANTALOUPE

Half the reason I love to grill duck is that I get to trim it beforehand and gather a nice collection of duck fat that will make a grand appearance at some unsuspecting future meal and just blow it up. The other reason is because, well, it's duck, and duck is tasty as hell. If you have a lengthy bacon résumé, those skills will translate rather nicely to duck. Both are very fatty and have a nice skin that can get super crunchy. For a spectacular affect, pair your crispy-skinned grilled duck with something cool and luscious, like cantaloupe.

SERVES 2 TO 4

1 duck, approximately 2 pounds

3 cloves garlic, crushed and minced

2 tablespoons honey

1 tablespoon peanut oil

1 tablespoon ground chili pepper or paprika

2 teaspoons coarse salt

½ cup fresh cilantro leaves for garnish

½ cantaloupe, sliced ¼ inch thick

EQUIPMENT

Spray bottle filled with water

Basting brush

1. Bring the grill up to medium heat and the duck to room temperature.

2. Cut duck in half lengthwise.

3. Pat skin dry with a towel, and gently separate it from the body, enough to insert as much of the crushed garlic as possible.

4. Place the duck, skin side down, over medium heat, and grill it for 6 minutes, or until it is crispy and the skin is golden brown. Keep a spray bottle of water on hand to squirt down any flare-ups. Make sure the spray is more of a mist than a jet, though, since a jet of water can shoot ash all over your bird.

5. Flip the duck and grill it, bone side down, for 10 minutes. Meantime, whisk together the honey, oil, chili pepper or paprika, and salt.

6. Brush the skin side of the duck with the honey mixture, and flip it so that the skin side is down. Move the duck slightly off the direct heat. Grill it for 2 minutes, and then paint the meaty side of the duck with the honey mixture and flip it over again. Repeat, so the duck cooks 4 to 6 minutes total per side.

7. Garnish with cilantro leaves, and serve with thin slices of cantaloupe alongside the duck.

GRILLED CHICKEN CALZONE

A boneless chicken thigh laid out flat is big enough to be stuffed and sewn up. With tomato sauce, cheese, and mushrooms and some caramelized onions it begins to resemble a calzone. The crispy skin on the outside works well with vegetables and cheese on the inside.

SERVES 2 TO 4

¼ cup white onions, diced

2 boneless, skin-on chicken thighs about 1½ pounds

1 teaspoon kosher salt

6 shitake mushrooms, with stem on

2 tablespoons olive oil

1 cup mozzarella

1 cup cherry tomatoes, quartered

EQUIPMENT

2 wood skewers soaked for 1 to 2 hours

1. Caramelize the onions, and set aside until ready to use.

2. Bring grill to medium-low heat.

3. Bring chicken to room temperature and pat it dry.

4. Lightly salt the meat side of the chicken, and lay it flat over direct heat. Grill for 10 minutes. Do not flip the chicken over during this time.

5. Meanwhile, coat the mushrooms with olive oil and salt, and place them on the grill. Be sure to leave the stems on to help keep the mushrooms from falling through the grates.

6. Remove all the ingredients from the heat. Lay the chicken out flat with the raw skin side down. Cover the cooked meat side of the chicken with the cheese, tomatoes, and grilled mushrooms.

7. Fold the chicken in half, sealing in the vegetables and cheese. Using a skewer, close up the open side by passing it through the skin in a zig zag motion.

8. Grill the chicken over medium-low heat for 20 minutes, flipping it once after about 10 minutes.

6

SEAFOOD

Four of us are crammed onto a small, 15-foot wooden motorboat. The plexiglass windscreens have been removed and thrown into a corner. Jackie, the captain, was named after an elder woman who died just before his birth. That is the naming custom in his Inuit village of Pangnirtung—or just "Pang"—in the Canadian territory of Nunavut. People in this arctic community may still gaze at him, trying to get a glimpse or a gesture of an old grandma whose soul is thought to live on in his man's body. To me, however, Jackie is a bad-ass dude—stout, black-haired with a bristly moustache. Here, at sea, he holds a greasy elephant gun loaded with rounds of .375 magnum bullets. Each is literally the size of a magic marker, and dozens of them are scattered about the dashboard.

The motor idles, emanating small ripples into the surface of the glassy sea. Everyone's eyes are locked on the horizon. An iceberg floats by. The most beautiful sunset has been lighting the surrounding snow-covered mountains for hours. It's 2 a.m., and through a series of random circumstances, I am on a whale hunt in the middle of the Arctic Ocean wearing just a sweatshirt and wet pants. I had been char fishing with some Inuit at a remote camp when the word came in that a herd of beluga whales had been spotted in Cumberland Sound, and here we wait, feverishly.

I do not condone the killing of whales, but this is different. Though I am anguished by what I see, I can't help but feel some relief that there are at least a few places on this planet where age-old culture and traditions have not been completely wiped out. And, after all, whale meat has sustained communities like Jackie's for 5,000 years.

After an intense four hours, the hunt is over. The whale, harpooned, floats on its side by the boat. Huge blast holes pepper its beautiful ivory skin. Jackie maneuvers his boat in the surf and gracefully brings it to a rest on a rock island the size of a baseball diamond. Grabbing the rope of the harpoon, the four of us drag the behemoth out of the surf as best as we can, and the hunters immediately begin to break down the whale.

Nowhere is the politics of food so palpable than in the Canadian arctic. Food preparation and consumption are based on geography, religion, rituals, myths, superstitions, and politics.

In Pang everyone shares food. If someone gets lucky and kills a few seals, he will chop one into quarters, place one of the pieces in a garbage bag, walk across town to an elder's home or to a family with a new baby, and leave the hunk of raw meat on a piece of cardboard on the living room floor. Talk about social graces! Imagine the horror this would provoke in a New Jersey suburb, crystal swans adorning the mantel.

Ringed seal is the most common source of food

in Pangnirtung. The entire animal is consumed. The meat is shared among the community; the skins are made into gloves, jackets, and boots; and even the bones are used for toys and trinkets. Kids in Pang actually play with these things, although they prefer digital gadgets.

Thankfully, hunting is alive and well in the arctic, and many families try their best to ignore the growing presence of southern influences by "going out on the land." I've made several trips to the north and had the privilege of going out on the land. Families will pack up their boats, canvas tents, portable stoves, and leave town, sometimes for months, to live in the wilderness hunting, fishing, and enjoying *inusutiavik*—the good life.

Fishing, too, is a common activity. Fishing in the arctic from the shores of an Inuit village feels like fishing before humans ruled. I always felt that I could actually catch a monster char there, and people do. I'd get up early, consider the tides and rock formations. I'd fuss with lures and weights. I'd sneak around the water's edge like a cat. I'd fish for hours, and then, from nowhere, a bunch of little six-year-old brats with boogers in their noses and missing teeth would come scampering around the shoreline, fighting over a single, broken, two-foot rod. They would cast, and—*boom!*—a big old char. The kids would push one another around, fall into the water, and laugh. One kid would be lugging around her dirt bike, banging it along the ancient boulders and throwing rocks into the water. But again and again, the kids would catch fish. What could I do but watch and learn and appreciate that I clearly have nothing on these kids?

Late one afternoon, I went out in a kayak with another southerner (anyone who is not from the arctic is considered a southerner) and crossed the mile-wide fjord—300-feet deep, emerald green, cold, and calm. Killer whales, bowhead whales, and Greenland sharks inhabit these waters. Our mission: to fish the stream head on the other side of the fjord, where there would be no competition from first-graders. We fished for hours. We crossed back at 1 a.m. having caught nothing.

As we approached the town, we could see a group of young children, ranging from five to ten years old, in the distance. They wielded sticks with nails and shards of broken glass taped to the ends. They'd climbed up on shipping containers, where we could see their varying heights silhouetted against the sunset. They watched us paddle into the marina from their perch, and there, strung from ropes, were a dozen arctic char.

This *Lord of the Flies* scenario played out every night in the village. There, in the summer months, kids are free to leave the confines of their homes and learn the ways of their hunter society in a manner that would leave most American parents paralyzed with absolute horror. (Eventually, I did catch several char and

cooked them on the hills with the only available fuel—heather moss.)

The days in Pang revolve mostly around the tides in the summer months, when the sun shines 24/7. At low tide we check the nets for char; at high tides we take out the boats to hunt for seal or whatever else is still allowable within the strict quota system. There is no TV, no video, no news media—just pure nature and humanity. Stress is gone. This is *inusutiavik*.

HERB-BLAZED ARCTIC CHAR

Cooking char on the shoreline in Pang, we are hundreds of miles above the treeline. Old pallets, washed ashore from various deliveries, are the only available source of wood, but once they burn down to coals they provide a good base on which to layer flavorful heather moss from the surrounding hills. Stones can be used to keep the fish off the fire and protect it from the wind.

SERVES 2

2 tablespoons unsalted butter

1 arctic char, 1½ pounds, cleaned and gutted

2 large bundles of fresh herbs—such as thyme, basil, rosemary (in moderation), bay leaves, tarragon, and so forth, about 1 bushel altogether

Coarse sea salt

1 lemon, sliced (optional)

1. Bring the grill to medium-high heat.

2. Meanwhile, in a small saucepan melt the butter, being careful not to burn it. Set it aside.

3. Rinse the fish and pat it dry. Stuff the cavity with a handful of the herbs. Then brush the exterior of the fish with the melted butter and sprinkle the fish with salt.

4. Grab half of the remaining bundle of herbs and make it into a dense nest.

5. Lay the nest over direct coals and place the fish on top of the nest. Cook it for 10 minutes, until the herbs have burned to ashes. Remove the fish and brush off any ash. Place the remaining bundle of herbs over the fire, flip the fish over, and lay it back on the herb nest.

6. Cook the fish for another 10 minutes.

7. Lift the fish from the embers with a wide spatula or knife, clean it off, and plate it.

8. Remove the herbs from the cavity.

9. Garnish with lemon slices, if using.

PASILLA SHRIMP KEBABS

I once spent two weeks holed up at the Intercontinental Hotel in Abu Dhabi binge-watching the first three seasons of *Game of Thrones*. Because of jet lag at night, I couldn't sleep, so I would watch an episode; then I *really* couldn't sleep. This happened every night until I watched all three seasons.

By day, I would stumble around like a zombie, sweating profusely (115°F in the shade!). I would take a taxi to the Mina fish market to eat prawns for lunch. These shrimps were enormous—U2 or U4—meaning that there were two or four of them to the pound, unlike the standard 20/25 to the pound in U.S supermarkets. These prehistoric sea creatures were grilled right in front of me and served with a smoky Middle Eastern spice mix. When I got back to New York I went straight to work making my own recipe for it.

> **SERVES 4**

¼ cup Lex's Pasilla Salt (page 141)

2 tablespoons melted butter

½ to 1 pound cleaned shrimp, 21/25

EQUIPMENT

About 5 to 10 wood skewers, depending on the size of the shrimp.

Basting brush

1. Prepare Lex's Pasilla Salt; set aside until ready for use.

2. Bring coals to medium-high heat.

3. Meanwhile, in a saucepan melt the butter. Set it aside until ready for use.

4. When the grill is ready, add 5 chilled shrimp to each skewer, making sure there is ½ inch between each shrimp. There is no need to soak the skewers first, as the shrimp cook very quickly.

5. Paint the shrimp with the melted butter, and sprinkle them generously with the pasilla salt.

6. Grill the shrimp for 1 minute, and then flip the skewers. Continue to grill the shrimp until they look opaque.

7. Serve immediately.

> PASILLA SHRIMP KEBABS PAIR WELL WITH SLICED MANGOS AS WELL AS A COCONUT CURRY SAUCE (SEE RECIPE ON PAGE 155).

SHRIMP SIZES, COUNTS, AND WEIGHT

Shrimp are identified by a number like 21/25, which means there are approximately 21 to 25 shrimp per pound. Large shrimp are identified by a number such as U8, which means there are 8 or fewer shrimp per pound.

CRUNCHY BLACK BRANZINO WITH LEMONATO SAUCE

When you're not looking to shower your guests in bacon sausages, this light and flaky dish just might fit the bill. It's delicate, healthy, sustainable, beautiful, and goes well with many different sauces and textures. Branzino is a fish that lends itself well to grilling, although some TLC is required during the flipping process.

SERVES 2

1 whole branzino, approximately 1½ pounds, cleaned and gutted

1 cup Black Panko

½ cup Lemonato Sauce (page 161)

1 lemon, thinly sliced

2 tablespoons olive oil, divided

1 tablespoon medium-sized sea salt

½ teaspoon red chile flakes

EQUIPMENT

Steel-bristle grill brush

Tongs

Paper towels

Vegetable oil for cleaning the grill, Kosher salt for cleaning the grill

Basting brush

Thin, metal spatula

1. Refrigerate the fish before grilling.

2. Prepare the Black Panko and the Lemonado Sauce in advance.

3. Bring the grill to high heat.

4. Clean the grill well, following the instructions on page 128.

5. Stuff the cavity of the fish with the lemon slices.

6. Brush the outside of the fish, on both sides, with 1 tablespoon of the olive oil, and sprinkle it with sea salt.

7. Once the grill is piping hot, wipe the grates one final time with a clean paper towel doused in vegetable oil. Lay the fish on the grill. Do not touch it for 3 minutes.

8. After 3 minutes, gently flip the fish with a thin, metal spatula and grill it for another 3 minutes. The fish is done when the eyes are powdery white.

9. Remove the fish from the grill. Gently brush it with the reserved tablespoon of olive oil, and then either roll it in the Black Panko to cover it completely or lay the fish on top of the Black Panko.

10. Serve the fish with Lemonato Sauce.

GRILLED MANGO LOBSTER PO'BOYS

Spending a number of years living in Mexico City, I was always taken aback by how classist Mexican society is. If you're in the upper class, you will make a point of making sure everyone knows it (cardigan sweater tied around the neck, polo shirt, khakis, leather loafers, and so on). I thought strutting around with an air of entitlement went extinct with cheesy 1980s' movies (the preppies in *Nerds* comes to mind). On the other hand, in the United States, a millionaire media start-up kid can be best friends with a Starbucks barista—to me, that seems more a matter of chemistry than class.

In the same democratic vein, this dish loves decadent, fresh Maine lobster just as much as it loves Big Bertha's Bargain Basement mayo. In the end, chemistry reigns.

> SERVES 4

1 lobster, approximately 1 pound

¼ cup mayonnaise

1 teaspoon classic yellow mustard

1 teaspoon smoked paprika

¼ seedless cucumber, peeled and diced

½ fresh, ripe mango, diced

⅛ cup parsley, chopped finely

1 teaspoon capers, whole or chopped (optional)

4 buttered white hot dog buns

1 tablespoon butter

1. Bring the grill to medium heat.

2. Grill the whole lobster over direct heat for 10 minutes, flipping it once after 5 minutes.

3. Mix together the mayonnaise, mustard, paprika, cucumber, mango, parsley, and capers.

4. Remove all the meat from the lobster.

5. Coarsely chop all of the lobster meat and combine it with the mayonnaise mixture.

6. Butter and grill the hot dog buns, spreading them open, insides down, over medium-low heat until they're golden brown.

7. Stuff the toasted buns with the lobster mixture and serve them to eager fans.

GRILLED LITTLENECK CLAMS

Clams are fun to grill because they are little rascals that just won't fall through the grates, no matter how many opportunities you give them. Their delicacy absorbs all the character of your grill as well, and then you douse them in butter and eat them. All reward, no loss. Since the cooking part is easy, I spend all my time complicating things in the sauce department. Browned Butter with Tarragon adds some sass without stealing the show.

SERVES 2

Browned Butter with Tarragon (page 151)

2 dozen littleneck clams, roughly 2 pounds

2 tablespoons Pecorino Romano shavings

1 lemon

1. Prepare the Browned Butter with Tarragon Sauce in advance. Set it aside until ready to use.

2. Clean the clams by soaking them in cold water for 15 minutes. Only cook clams that are closed.

3. Bring the grill to medium-high heat.

4. Arrange the clams on the grill over direct heat. Grill the clams over medium-high heat for 4 minutes.

5. Slice the lemons and quickly grill the slices. Remove the clams and lemon slices from the grill, discard any clams that don't open. Transfer the clams to a warm serving dish, and sprinkle them with Pecorino Romano shavings.

6. Let the clams sit for 30 seconds; then pour the Browned Butter with Tarragon Sauce over them and serve.

SCALLOPS WITH LECHE DE TIGRE

Landing in Cuzco, Peru, you are greeted with a long line of wheelchairs. An ominous sight indeed! At 12,000 feet, the altitude of the city is nothing you can't get used to, but if you've just spent the last few days down at sea level and perhaps enjoying the nightlife of Lima, you might want to just sit down and wheel yourself over to the luggage claim. Peruvians love their ceviche, and so do I! It's heavy on lime, orange juice, and aji pepper. It's not thick and tomato-y like its Mexican counterpart. But what really gets me is the combination of ceviche and fire. A particularly special dish is trout in a *leche de tigre* sauce: a spicy, lime-based sauce used for cooking with acid. The fish is later covered with salt and sugar and hit with a blowtorch. Oh Ma Gawd! Crispy caramelized? Yes! Spicy and zesty? Check! This dish has got it all going on. I have taken inspiration from trout in *leche de tigre* and applied it to scallops on the grill. Enjoy it as irresponsibly as possible.

SERVES 2 TO 4

1½ cups *Leche de Tigre* Sauce (page 161)

8 fresh jumbo scallops

2 to 3 large limes

¼ cup salt

¼ cup white sugar

Orange zest for garnish (optional)

EQUIPMENT

8 empty soup cans or a large pan lid

1. Prepare the *Leche de Tigre* Sauce.

2. Gently toss the scallops in ½ cup of the *Leche de Tigre* Sauce and put them on a plate in the refrigerator for 1 hour.

3. Bring the grill up to very high temperature.

4. Cut 8 slices of lime ¼ inch thick, making sure each slice is large enough to serve as a plate for one scallop.

5. In a small bowl, thoroughly mix the salt and sugar. Remove the scallops from the refrigerator, and blot them dry. Sprinkle each scallop with the salt and sugar combo.

6. Place the 8 lime slices on the grill, and immediately put a scallop on top of each slice. Keep the slices close together over direct heat so your lid can cover all of them, or leave enough space between the slices so that each one can be covered by an empty soup can, without the cans touching each other.

7. Grill the scallops at high heat for about 8 minutes. The caramelized salt/sugar combo is what makes this dish! The soup cans keep any uprising heat next to the scallops. Another great trick is to keep a charcoal chimney blazing and then gently hold each scallop (using tongs) over the intense flames.

8. Plate the scallops, and pour the remaining cup of the *Leche de Tigre* Sauce around them.

9. If you'd like, garnish the scallops with some orange zest.

AFRICAN-STYLE SNAPPER

Kribi is a beach town in Cameroon known for its seafood, and the fact that it's haunted. At night, the markets have no light except for the coals in the grills and the moon reflecting off the ocean. This dish is what is served at all the stands. It originated in Ivory Coast but has long since been adopted by all of its neighbors. The fish is served alongside *attieke*, ground and fermented cassava that can be found in African markets and resembles a very fine couscous. If you have a chance, find some and pair it with this recipe.

SERVES 3 OR 4

¼ cup Chile de Arbol Salsa (page 153) or hot sauce of your choice

1 red snapper, approximately 3 pounds

1 tablespoon coarsely crushed white peppercorns

1 teaspoon kosher salt

1 teaspoon garlic powder

¼ cup canola oil for basting

1 tomato, diced

1 small onion, diced

EQUIPMENT

Steel-bristle grill brush

Tongs

Paper towels

Peanut or grape seed oil for grates

Kosher salt

Mortar and pestle

1. Prepare the Chile de Arbol Salsa (if using) in advance. Set aside until ready to serve.

2. Clean the grill well, following the instructions on page 128.

3. Bring the grill up to high temperature, and wipe the grates one final time with a clean paper towel doused in peanut or grape seed oil.

4. In a mortar and pestle, roughly crush peppercorns. Mix with salt and garlic powder.

5. Clean and dry snapper and make 2 to 3 score marks on each side with a sharp knife. Coat the mix of pepper, salt and garlic powder.

6. Grill the fish for 4 minutes on each side. The fish will be will done when the meat becomes flaky and opaque.

7. Serve alongside chopped tomato, onion, and Chile de Arbol Salsa (or hot sauce).

FISH NEED IT CLEAN

Being obsessive-compulsive is not a disorder when it comes to cleaning grill grates for fish. It's a necessity. Fish requires perfectly cleaned and oiled grates so that it does not stick. To get the job done, you will need a good steel-bristle grill brush, long-handled tongs, paper towels, vegetable oil, and kosher salt. Fire it up, and once the grill starts to get hot, scrub and clean it very well with the steel-bristle brush. Using long-handled tongs, continue to clean and scrub the grill with a paper towel soaked in vegetable oil and sprinkled with kosher salt.

GRAVLAX

Gravlax is salt- and sugar-cured salmon, cut thin and usually served on crackers. Though the fish is not grilled, it does pair harmoniously and virtuously with coal-baked bread and pickled red onions. Because it is so light and fresh, I like to serve it at my barbecues.

▷ MAKES 20 TO 30 THIN SLICES FOR SNACKS ◁

1 large fillet of wild, fresh chinook salmon, about 2 pounds

½ cup white sugar

½ cup kosher salt

1 tablespoon ground white pepper

1 teaspoon ground juniper berries (optional)

1 large bunch of fresh dill (approximately 3 cups)

1 habanero pepper, thinly sliced (optional)

1 shot of brandy (needed only if your fish is not of superior quality or freshness)

1. Prepare the salmon 3 days before you plan to use it. Rinse the fillet and pat it dry.

2. Mix together the sugar, salt, pepper, and juniper berries, if you're using them, and pour them on a plate.

3. Roll the salmon in the sugar, salt, and pepper mix, making sure to coat both sides evenly and thoroughly.

4. Lay the salmon in a sheet of plastic wrap, and tuck the dill and habanero slices around the fish on all sides.

5. Add the brandy to the fish, if desired, and roll it tightly several times over in the plastic wrap.

6. Put the wrapped fish in a tightly sealed container, and place it in the refrigerator for 3 days.

7. When you are ready to serve it, remove the fish from its wrappings and rinse it off.

8. Cut the fish at an angle into thin slices and serve it with crackers and cream cheese, or just eat it as is.

GINGER GLAZED SALMON ON A STICK

Ray Mears is always the calm and collected voice of outdoor chefs. And he knows the wild. Watching him grill salmon in primitive ways is always an inspiration and gets me thinking about backyard applications. In this recipe, I like to cut the salmon filets 1 inch wide with the skin on and skewer them lengthwise. . For the backyard grill, use either metal or wooden skewers, and for a campfire, use a longer stick—the same kind you'd use to toast marshmallows.

> MAKES 4 SALMON STICKS

2 tablespoons Ginger Glaze (page 139)

½ pound fillet of kings salmon (aka chinook salmon)

1 teaspoon Maldon salt

2 tablespoons melted butter

EQUIPMENT

Basting brush

Aluminum foil

4 wood skewers, 10 inches long

1. Prepare the Ginger Glaze and set it aside.

2. Bring the grill to medium-high heat.

3. Cut the salmon fillet into long, 1-inch-wide strips. Pat them dry and sprinkle them with the salt.

4. Measure out 2 tablespoons of Ginger Glaze, reserving the remainder to serve with the grilled fish. Mix the melted butter with the 2 tablespoons of Ginger Glaze.

5. With the salmon strips laying skin side down, brush the flesh side of the strips with the butter and glaze mixture.

6. Drive the skewers lengthwise through the salmon strips.

7. Optional: Use a brick or aluminum foil bridge to prop up one side of the skewers so the fish sits right above the grill grates without touching them.

8. Grill the skewers for 5 to 7 minutes total, while rotating them constantly.

9. The salmon is done when it becomes flakey. Serve it with the reserved Ginger Glaze.

7

RUBS & SALTS

Roman warriors were often paid with salt for two reasons: because it was worth its weight in gold and because it tastes good on dinner. Because of this, the word *salary* stems from the Latin word for salt. And just like a salary, salt makes everything better.

Making your own salts and rubs is one of the easiest and best ways to add flavor to dishes and make them your own. They're also incredibly cheap and quick to make, and you control the elements—the intensity of heat and flavor. What's more, with some nice packaging, salts and rubs make awesome gifts. Seriously, who doesn't like a nice bag of salt from a friend?

THE SPICY LIFE

If food is a reflection of culture, spices say a lot about you and how much fun you're willing to get yourself into. Take our dear neighbors, Mexico and Canada: In one we, find things like sexy salsa dancing, telenovelas, mariachis, cenote diving, goat head tacos, and tequila; in the other, we find, well, not so much.

Spicy peppers originated in Mexico and were first introduced to Europeans by Columbus. From there, chiles traveled the world, and depending on the soil in which they were planted, they took on different flavors and intensities. Nowhere have I seen such profound integration of chiles into food as in Mexico. It is interwoven into the country's identity. And the variety is unbelievable. Peppers are used fresh, boiled, fried, smoked, dried, pickled—you name it—and the variants often go by different names. For example, chipotles are actually ripe, red jalapeños that have been smoked for about a week.

DINNER IN DOUALA

It's 95 degrees and humid in Douala, Cameroon. We slouch on the outdoor patio on torn "pleather" couches that surround a table covered with bush meat, smoked skate fish, shrimp, and snails. A bowl of liquefied yucca accompanies the meats and is passed around, along with a bowl of water for washing our hands.

It's also 3 a.m., and I've been slurping down lukewarm beers for hours and am quite ready for bed. My in-laws will stay up until seven in the morning. They're not even drinking—they're just straight up chatting. Apparently time in Cameroon in Central Africa does not have the same urgency as it does elsewhere. This goes for meals, family talks, and visits. In New York, whenever we invite a Cameroonean family over for dinner, we invite them for lunch at noon. Six hours later they arrive, apologizing for being late. I assure them they are right on time.

In Douala, our porch has a single, crooked, fluorescent bulb that buzzes and flickers. No one cares. Beyond its hard light there is total darkness. Sometimes, just a few feet away in the darkness I hear footsteps or a snippet of conversation from passersby. My wife, Gladys, and her sisters are arguing over family matters. At one point the conversation gets so heated that everyone stands up pointing and shouting over one another. When they notice my concern, they stop and immediately break out in laughter.

By day the city streets come alive, like a scene from *Beyond Thunderdome*. Walls of dust rise as huge groups of apocalyptic bikers swarm throughout the streets every which way. At each intersection

I imagine Tina Turner, hoisted high in the air on a steel plank screaming, "Two men enter, one man leaves!" Small two-stroke bikes sit three passengers, sometimes four. On one of them, a guy is eating a sandwich, a lady is talking on her phone, and a third passenger, a young kid, is hanging on, clutching a ceiling fan; while the driver, seemingly bored and totally unfrazzled, swerves through the utter madness of it all, dodging potholes that could literally swallow a washing machine. Meanwhile, giant dump trucks, the kind featured in those kids' books called *Giant Dump Trucks*, share the dusty streets, along with 18-wheelers, herds of cattle, train tracks, and a million cars. Everyone is vying for space and an opportunity to advance. There are no stop signs, no stop lights, no apparent order. Some pedestrians make quick breaks for it, others calmly balance hundreds of perfectly stacked limes in an inverted trash can lid on their head, and dilly dally through the madness I mean, what could possibly go wrong here? When was it all going to come crashing down?

The markets are just as intense . . . in a different way: Herbs like *rondelle écrasées*, *mbongo*, *cancan*, *ndole*, yucca, snails, live chickens, dead cows, bush meat, dead dogs . . . are packed into stands covered with tarps in narrow alleys. In them, you'll also find African robes, sandals, and wallets for sale. The ground is muddy, and people's feet are bare. Occasionally, here and there, you'll spot pools of blood in the market . . . . And every single person there is staring at me. Many people just stop what they are doing and stand up and silently point, as if out of duty. Others matter-of-factly shrug it off. Others break out into intense debates. Do I act like I don't notice? Do I just say hi to everyone and make a speech? What the hell do I say? Well, of course I do the worst possible thing I can do: At this moment I decide to buy something. What? I dunno, Anything! The hair-on leather wallet: "How much?" Two thousand cefas ($3). As I reach into my pocket to grab cash, the audience erupts into laughter. Being an out-of-towner and woefully inept at local graces, I forgot to bargain. Given the opportunity, I might have mentioned that I thought the price was fair, even a steal. I could say maybe that it would also appear rude to come in from one of the richest places on Earth and try to nickel-and-dime some of the poorest people.

The spices in Cameroon are like nothing I have ever tasted anywhere else, ever. Their aroma and taste evoke deep, earthy notes of peppers, bitterness, smoke, and something that can only be described as spicy nutmeg. Out of pure necessity, meats are used very sparingly, and they're doused with intense flavor from a range of spices and herbs and served alongside large portions of yucca and cassava in various forms. A dish of thin strips of intensely flavored meat goes a long way, although there is not much of it to go around, and the quality can be questionable. But with plenty of spices, it can be rich, complex, and utterly divine!

DARK RUB

This all-purpose rub is deep, sophisticated, and awesome on lamb! The cumin reminds me of the intensely flavored, spicy kebabs that are so popular in Xi'an, China, which usually feature beef, pork, fish or mutton. The allspice/herbes de Provence combo lends itself especially well to tender meats, such as fish. And, just like all rubs, blending this dark rub into a fine powder is best for smaller cuts that don't cook too long. Try a coarser salt, like Maldon, and larger bits of chiles and black pepper that can really take a beating and create a nice bark on larger cuts.

3 whole pasilla peppers

3 cloves garlic, peeled

1 tablespoon ground allspice

2 tablespoons black pepper

2 tablespoons salt

2 tablespoons dark brown sugar

1 tablespoon ground cumin

1 tablespoon herbes de Provence

1. Remove the stems and seeds from the pasilla peppers and dice them. Also dice the garlic and toast it and the diced peppers on low heat for 5 minutes or until they are dry.

2. If you are using whole allspice and peppercorns, crush them in a mortar and pestle until they are the desired size.

3. Add the salt, brown sugar, cumin, and herbes de Provence to the pan. Toast the mix on low heat for another 3 minutes.

4. If you want a finer blend, process all of the ingredients in a coffee grinder or crush them in a mortar and pestle until the mix is finely ground.

5. Store the rub in a glass jar with a lid.

GINGER GLAZE

Ginger is versatile and fresh. I don't recall eating it much as a kid, but then again it's a mature flavor and one that adds great dimension to every food that does not fall under the category of "simple comfort." When complexity is desired, ginger answers the call, and using it with honey adds a subdued sophistication.

⅓ cup fresh squeezed orange juice

3 tablespoons honey

1 or 2 tablespoons soy sauce

¼ teaspoon ground ginger

Apple cider vinegar (optional)

1. Mix the orange juice, honey, soy sauce, ginger, and vinegar in a small saucepan over high heat and reduce by one-third. If the mixture becomes too tacky, loosen it with a tablespoon of apple cider vinegar.

GREEN MICHELADA SALT

This zesty and refreshing green-colored salt is awesome with cold beer or tequila. As a seasoning, it also works spectacularly on chicken (see, for example, Skinless Chicken Breasts with Lemonato Sauce on page 97), but it should be added toward the end of the cooking time, since its flavors are gentle and fresh and will burn off with too much heat.

1 tablespoon fresh lime zest (about 5 limes)

2 teaspoons grated ginger

3 tablespoons kosher salt

2 tablespoons dried cilantro or ground coriander

1 tablespoon garlic powder

1. Zest the limes with a microplane until you have about 1 tablespoon of fine zest.

2. Mix the lime zest with the ginger, salt, dried cilantro (or ground coriander), and garlic powder.

3. Store the mixture at room temperature or in the fridge in a sealed jar.

THE HOLY RUB

MAKES ½ CUP

You think you've seen it all, but after watching the Na Nach in action you may as well hang up your *shtreimel* because nothing will ever surprise you ever again. The Na Nach sect of Breslover Hasidim are party animals who bounce around out of sync to techno music on the streets of Tel Aviv, their *payos* flailing about like the arms of a drowning victim.

I first witnessed this miracle of dance outside the Sabich Tchernikovsky, one of the best spots in Tel Aviv to sample Iraqi–Israeli street food, and wholeheartedly took it as a sign of divine sandwiches, which of course it was. This recipe was inspired by the one I had at the Tchernikovsky: grilled sweet eggplant and hard-boiled eggs, layered with hummus and sprinkled with za'atar in a fresh, hot pita.

4 tablespoons Maldon salt

2 tablespoons za'atar

2 tablespoons light brown sugar

2 tablespoons ground cinnamon

1½ tablespoons ground turmeric

1. Thoroughly mix the salt, za'atar, brown sugar, cinnamon, and turmeric. Store the mixture at room temperature in a sealed jar.

LEX'S PASILLA SALT

In my office, I keep a jar of this stuff around to spruce up a boring lunch. The little gifts I package up usually consist of this rub. When I had the hairbrained idea to start the world's largest dry-rub empire and rule it with an iron fist, this was to be the cornerstone of my dynasty.

3 large pasilla peppers

2 fresh chiles de arbol

1 tablespoon fresh ground white peppercorns

1 tablespoon garlic powder

2 tablespoons kosher salt

1 tablespoon light brown sugar, or 1 tablespoon granulated sugar

1. Lightly toast the chiles over the grill or the flames on your stove, or grill them until you smell the pepper aroma. Keep the heat low and rotate the chiles constantly. You don't want to burn these.

2. Once the chiles begin to expand from the heat and become more aromatic, remove them from the heat. Then remove the stem and seeds.

3. Crush the chiles and white pepper in a coffee grinder, or use a mortar and pestle. (You can also use a couple clean rocks to do the job.)

4. Mix the crushed chiles with the garlic powder, salt, and brown sugar.

5. Option: Granulated sugar can be used instead of brown sugar, but it won't cake as easily as brown sugar and it will create a different texture.

6. Store the mixture in a sealable glass canning jar.

PICKLING SALT

Pickling can brighten the flavor, reduce bitterness, add sweetness, and enhance the crispiness of just about anything. This pickling salt is great for cucumbers, hot and sweet peppers, red onions, and heirloom carrots (as well as just about any other vegetable you can think of).

3 tablespoons iodized salt

½ cup castor sugar (or just throw ½ cup of white sugar in a coffee grinder and blend it until it resembles talc)

2 to 4 dried bay leaves, roughly cut

5 to 10 dried allspice berries, semi-crushed

½ teaspoon gently crushed black pepper

½ teaspoon coriander seeds, lightly crushed

2 cups apple cider vinegar

4 cups cold water

1. Thoroughly mix the salt, sugar, crushed bay leaves, allspice berries, pepper, and coriander seed. Store them in a sealed jar at room temperature.

2. When you're ready, mix the dry ingredients with the apple cider vinegar and cold water, and pickle the food for 8 to 48 hours.

SALT & SAGE

Making your own flavored salts is a big game changer. Making a batch is easy and it can last for months. All you have to do is toast up some herbs and garlic, and then crush, chop, or blend the mix to the desired chunkiness. Mix it all with some salt and you're good to go. Toasting the herbs and salt can be done in the grill—on a rock or in a little pan—where the mix can pick up some great smoke flavors and color, as well.

MAKES 1 CUP

4 cloves garlic

1 tablespoon fresh sage

4 tablespoons Maldon salt

1. Mince the garlic and sage and toast them on low heat in little pan for 5 minutes, stirring constantly.

2. Blend or crush the garlic/sage mixture to the desired fineness.

3. Gently mix in the salt.

4. Store the mixture in a glass jar with a lid and keep it in the refrigerator.

SMOKY RUB

This rub is bold and virtuous! It gives meaning and purpose to the bland flavors one might encounter with lean white meats. The rub can also easily be made fine and granular for small cuts of meat or nice and chunky for huge cuts you want to grill on a spit.

MAKES 1 CUP

2 large dried ancho chiles

2 tablespoons garlic powder

2 tablespoons fresh ground white pepper

2 tablespoons kosher salt

1 tablespoon light brown sugar

1. Thoroughly mix the chiles, garlic powder, pepper, salt, and brown sugar. Store them at room temperature in a sealed jar.

SWEDISH SALT

The combination of dill and allspice with the salt in this mix gives it aromatic and earthy qualities that pair beautifully with mussels and shellfish, and work nicely in a pickling brine, as well. To make a great dipping sauce, add 1 teaspoon of this salt mix to a few tablespoons of melted butter.

2 tablespoons kosher salt

2 tablespoons dried dill

1 tablespoon ground allspice

1 tablespoon white pepper

1 tablespoon ground juniper berries (optional)

1. Thoroughly mix the kosher salt, dill, allspice, white pepper, and, if desired, juniper berries. Store them at room temperature in a sealed jar.

SWEET TARRAGON SALT

Mixing some fresh herbs with salt and toasting it results is some fine aromas. Tarragon salt is great combined with butter and used on lean white meats. It also plays nice, I find, with brown sugar and allspice.

4 cloves fresh garlic, minced

2 tablespoons fresh tarragon

¾ cup kosher salt

1 tablespoon ground black pepper

2 tablespoons light brown sugar

1. Finely dice, chop, or blend the garlic and tarragon into the desired size.

2. Slowly and gently toast the mix in pan over a smoky grill.

3. Thoroughly combine the toasted garlic/tarragon mixture with the salt, pepper, and sugar. Then store the mixture at room temperature in a sealed jar.

8

MARINADES, SALSAS, SAUCES & TOPPINGS

Matsui is an elderly lady who took me in to her home in Kyoto, Japan, for several days as a favor to a friend of a friend of a friend. I spoke no Japanese and she spoke no English. There were many rules, and her face was frozen in a permanent smile as she demonstrated them. The smile became more and more ominous as the rules increased. Take for example the rule pertaining to slippers.

The traditional house in Kyoto has several rooms, all of which are separated by outdoor walkways. At first this seems very lovely, as the walkways are surrounded by beautifully manicured gardens. But soon the rule of the slippers—that is, *always leave your slippers at the door*—takes hold. This rule becomes an issue when, for example, you have to travel from your room to the bathroom. I would walk the few paces to the door, gently remove my bedroom slippers and arrange them neatly, slide open the delicate rice paper door without fist-holing it, step out into the walkway, put on the outdoor slippers designated for this particular walkway, walk a few paces to the bathroom door, change into my bathroom slippers, walk a single pace to the toilet, piss, shake, turn around, walk a step, change slippers for the outdoor walkway, walk a few paces, remove slippers and arrange them neatly, open the door, and put on bedroom slippers—piss mission accomplished! Oh wait . . . forgot your cell phone back on the toilet? That's really too bad for you. A single trip to the bathroom and back requires six changes of slippers. Imagine now that your destination is two rooms removed. How many changes of slippers then? But wait! This is only the first part of the slipper rule.

Part two: When leaving your slippers behind, you must arrange them to anticipate your return. Merely stopping at a door and stepping out of your slippers would be reckless, as when you return they will be facing the wrong direction! Luckily for the human race there is a solution! When arriving at the door, turn around and enter backward, stepping out of your slippers and leaving them facing you for your return. I spent my time in Kyoto changing slippers and walking through doorways backwards. This was a pitiful site, as this is not a maneuver I execute with grace.

The concept of *Wa* is paramount in Japan and dictates that collaboration and harmony are superior to self-interest. And the harmony, balance, and utter divinity of Japanese food, reflects this philosophy. Grilling allows for a bit of recklessness, but great sauces come from patience and measured steps. Where big steaks of meat and fish reflect the ego, simple sauces celebrate the *Wa*. Even a humble sauce—making a reduction, whisking ingredients, and subtle variations on dicing and grating—can have a big impact on a dish, giving it identity and direction.

BACON JELLY

This recipe can also be made with pork jowl, which, in my opinion is better than bacon, but is harder to find. This bacon jelly is heavy and intense—and I came up with it when I was exploring sauces for Esquire TV's *The Next Great Burger* contest, but it was just too much of a good thing. If bacon is a bandage, this stuff is the sexy nurse with the laughing gas.

MAKES ½ CUP

6 strips of bacon

2 tablespoons honey

¼ teaspoon herbes de Provence

¼ teaspoon allspice

1 tablespoon red wine (optional)

1. In a pan over medium heat, cook the bacon with the lid on, flipping and pouring out the rendered fat as you go. (Keep this nectar of the gods for some future use.)

2. Cook the bacon until it is crunchy, remove it from the pan, and crush it into small pieces with a paper towel.

3. Put the bacon back in the pan and reintroduce 1 tablespoon of the fat.

4. Add the honey to the pan, on medium heat, and stir briskly to incorporate the bacon and honey.

5. Add the herbes de Provence, allspice, and wine (if you're using it) and cook the mixture for 2 minutes, stirring constantly.

6. Serve! If there is anything left to refrigerate, put it in a sealed jar in the refrigerator.

BASIC BARBECUE SAUCE

This is a great basic recipe for making your own barbecue sauce. Make a great base with the tomatoes, onion, and garlic; then build on that with honey, vinegar, and spices. This recipe works really well on its own, but it also sets the stage for other embellishments, depending on your taste.

▶ MAKES 1 CUP

2 tablespoons olive oil

½ medium white onion. diced

1 medium-large tomato

2 cloves garlic

3 tablespoons honey

2.5 tablespoons apple cider vinegar

1 teaspoon cayenne

1 teaspoon black pepper

1 to 2 teaspoons kosher salt

1. In a small saucepan heat the olive oil, then caramelize the onion on low heat.

2. In a blender, puree the tomato and garlic.

3. In a separate saucepan, add tomato/garlic puree and reduce by ¼ over low heat.

4. Combine the caramelized onions and the tomato/garlic puree.

5. Mix in honey and vinegar.

6. This should be a creamy and smooth sauce without much action. Slowly mix in the cayenne, pepper, and salt. The cayenne will add spice, and the pepper with add intensity, so add slowly, taste often, and find the balance right for you.

BLACK PANKO

This recipe makes a very nice accompaniment for fish dishes. It adds color and texture, not to mention flavor. I like to use it in Crunchy Black Branzino with Lemonato Sauce (page 120).

▶ MAKES ABOUT 1 CUP

1 cup dark bread, like pumpernickel

1 to 2 tablespoons squid ink or cuttlefish ink

1. In a bowl, tear up 3 large ¼-inch-thick slices of pumpernickel bread.

2. Mix the bread with the squid (or cuttlefish) ink, incorporating it until the bread is black.

3. Gently toast the bread until it is very dry and brittle.

4. Crush the bread into small flakes.

BLUE ROUX

This sauce is super rich, heavy, and will make you obese overnight. But it's so good for the soul that it's worth it.

MAKES 1 CUP

2 tablespoons butter

1 tablespoon all-purpose flour

¾ cup warm milk

1 teaspoon blue cheese

Salt and pepper to taste

1. Melt the butter over medium-low heat.

2. Stir in the flour, and gently cook the mixture for 5 minutes.

3. Whisk in the warm milk, and continue cooking. Stir continuously until the consistency resembles gravy.

4. Mix in the blue cheese, and allow it to fully melt.

5. Add salt and pepper to your liking and serve.

6. The roux will keep in the refrigerator for a few days.

BROWNED BUTTER WITH TARRAGON

The gentle anise flavor of the tarragon and the fresh lime make this sauce lively and fragrant and absolutely perfect served over mussels, clams, and flaky white fish.

MAKES ABOUT ½ CUP

3 tablespoons unsalted butter

2 tablespoons fresh, loose tarragon

1 tablespoon fresh lemon juice

¼ teaspoon kosher salt

1. In a small sauce pan over medium heat, melt the butter.

2. Add the tarragon and simmer the mixture on medium heat until the butter begins to brown.

3. Remove the mixture from the heat.

4. Add the lemon juice and serve.

5. Season with salt as desired.

BUTTERMILK MARINADE

Buttermilk is sour and not buttery. It pairs terribly with cookies. Its virtue is its ability to tenderize chicken like nothing else – and make biscuits. Regular milk can be turned into buttermilk simply by adding a bit of vinegar or lime juice—or you can leave the milk out of the fridge for a couple days, although this method is a very bad idea. If buttermilk is the sour element in this easy and spectacular marinade, honey, paprika, and salt add sweet, spicy, and, well, salty notes to the mix.

> **MAKES 2 CUPS**

2 cups buttermilk

2 tablespoons honey

2 teaspoons ground paprika

1 teaspoon salt

1. Thoroughly mix the buttermilk, honey, paprika, and salt. Then store the mixture in a jar with a tight-fitting lid. This will keep in the refrigerator for 24 to 48 hours.

CHICKEN SAUSAGE GRAVY

Whenever I break down a chicken to make sausages (or any other dish), I make chicken stock. Then, whenever I have a terrible day and need a pick-me-upper, I go home and make gravy with it. Gravy IS the real reason for thanksgiving, not the turkey, or the giving of thanks. It's that good.

Bones from 4 chicken legs

3 cups water

$\frac{1}{4}$ cup white flour

1 cup milk

$\frac{1}{2}$ teaspoon kosher salt

1 teaspoon coarse black pepper

1 tablespoon sage

1. In a pot of boiling water, add the chicken bones left over from the preparation of the chicken for the sausages. Boil for 20 minutes.

2. Remove the bones from the liquid, add flour, and stir.

3. Cook for 5 minutes, stirring often.

4. In another small pot, warm the milk. Do not allow it to come to a boil.

5. When the milk is warm, add it to the ingredients in the other pot. Whisk until the ingredients are thoroughly blended.

6. Add salt, pepper, and sage.

CHILE DE ARBOL SALSA

This is the classic red salsa found throughout Mexico. It is deep in flavor, smoky, nutty, and spicy, and has a gorgeous orange color. It's a classic on tacos and provides a great balance with fresh herbs, onions, and pineapple.

MAKES ABOUT 1 CUP

½ cup canola oil

3 Roma (plum) tomatoes

¼ white onion

1 to 2 cloves garlic

2 chiles de arbol

1 guajillo chile

2 teaspoons salt

1. In a small metal saucepan, heat the oil over medium heat for 5 to 6 minutes.

2. Roughly chop the tomatoes, onion, and garlic, and add to the oil.

3. Break the tips off the arbol and guajillo peppers, and shake out the seeds. Add the chiles to the oil.

4. Lightly fry all ingredients until the peppers begin to lighten in appearance, roughly 5 minutes.

5. With a slotted spoon, scoop out all the vegetables and peppers from the oil and place them in a blender.

6. Pour in a little oil and blend the mixture for about 10 seconds. The result should be a thick salsa. Not too much oil is needed.

7. Add salt, a little at a time, tasting as you go.

CHIMICHURRI SAUCE

Just like the relishes in the United States and chutneys in India, chimichurris, originally from South America, are uncooked sauces made to accompany meat. At their heart a chimichurri is parsley and oil. Peppers and onions can be added to varying degrees for a wide range of flavors colors and textures.

> MAKES 1 CUP

1 habanero pepper

1 small white onion

1 bunch parsley (about ¼ cup chopped)

1 cubanelle pepper

½ cup olive oil

1. Chop the pepper onion, parsley, and pepper to the sizes you prefer. I always cut the habanero into the smallest pieces I can make with a razor-sharp knife. Nobody wants to bite into a big chunk of habanero.

2. Mix all ingredients with the oil, and store the mixture in a resealable glass jar in the refrigerator.

3. The chimichurri can be served immediately, but it tastes 10 times better the next day when the oil has had time to absorb all the flavors. In fact, after a couple of days, the vegetables and parsley can be strained out and the oil can be used for other dishes.

4. Chimichurri will keep in the refrigerator for a week or so in a sealed container. Bring it to room temperature before using it as a sauce.

COCONUT CURRY SAUCE

I have always associated curry sauce with all-you-can-eat Indian buffets, and that's a shame, because even though anything that is all-you-can-eat is fun, it's seldom a religious experience. My perception of curry changed, though, when I started eating Japanese green curry in small, choreographed, and measured dishes. The experience cast a new light on green curry as a highly sophisticated and delicate spice.

MAKES ABOUT 1 1/2 CUPS

½ white onion, finely diced

1 tablespoon olive oil

3 tablespoons Japanese green curry powder

1½ cups coconut milk

Pinch kosher salt

1. In a pan, add onion and olive oil. Cook on medium-low heat for roughly 15 minutes to caramelize.

2. Once the onions begin to brown, slowly stir in curry powder. Add a little extra olive oil if the mixture is dry. Cook for 5 more minutes.

3. Pour in coconut milk, stirring constantly and cook for 5 more minutes.

4. Add a pinch or two of salt to taste.

5. Make sure there's no powdery or granular texture to the curry powder. If there is, cook longer until the mixture is smooth.

6. Any leftover curry sauce will keep in the refrigerator for up to 1 week.

CUCUMBER AIOLI

MAKES 1 CUP

¾ cup mayonnaise

¼ cup cucumber cut into ⅛-inch cubes

½ teaspoon kosher salt

1. Mix mayonnaise, cucumber, and kosher until the ingredients are well blended.

2. Keep the mixture in a well-sealed jar in the refrigerator. This can keep up to 1 week.

EEL SAUCE

Whether you're crushing all-you-can-eat sushi, enjoying some hand-made *takoyaki,* or just snoozing on the couch, eel sauce will brighten your day. It is sweet, subtle, sophisticated, and makes a great glaze for steaks and fish. It can also be built upon in amazing ways. Here are the basics. Of course, you can achieve better results with a fine, unpasteurized soy sauce and quality sake, but this works.

MAKES ½ CUP

¼ cup sake

¼ cup soy sauce

¼ cup brown sugar

1 tablespoon thinly sliced ginger

1. Put all the ingredients in a small pan and mix them together.

2. Over medium-low heat, cook the mixture until it is reduced by half.

3. Remove the ginger with a fork or strainer and let the mixture cool.

4. You can paint eel sauce onto food with a small pastry brush or by placing it in a small plastic bag and tenderly cutting off a miniscule edge with a knife or scissors. Use the bag to squeeze out lines of eel sauce over a finished dish.

5. Note that this sauce almost always mixes well with a small amount of mayonnaise, which can also be squeezed onto foods using the plastic bag method.

6. Keep any leftover sauce in the refrigerator for a week or so in a covered jar.

EGG YOLK AIOLI

This aioli offers a great creamy component to any dish, and its deep yellow color is a thing of beauty. Mix the aioli with some chives or scallions and serve it with fish or pair it with some cool, fresh heirloom tomatoes. It also pairs great with relish or pickles on sliders, burgers, and dogs.

> MAKES ABOUT ¾ CUP

3 egg yolks

1 teaspoon creamy yellow mustard

½ cup mayonnaise

1 tablespoon olive oil

3 cloves garlic, diced

Juice of 1 Meyer lemon

¼ teaspoon Maldon salt

Freshly ground pepper (optional)

1. Place the egg yolks and mustard in a small bowl, and whisk them together.

2. Add the mayonnaise and olive oil to the egg yolk mixture, along with the garlic, and give it a thorough blend.

3. When the mixture has thickened, add lemon juice and salt. Mix thoroughly and serve. Add freshly ground paper, if you like.

4. Refrigerate any leftover aioli, but don't keep it for more than a day or two at the most.

USING EGGS IN SAUCES

Egg yolks add creaminess, color, and nutrients to any sauce. Other ways to use them:

- Raw egg yolks are super-smooth, easy to whisk, and full of nutrients. Many bodybuilders swear by them. And these days, there's little chance of getting salmonella.

- Pasteurized eggs have many of the benefits of raw eggs, but are ever so slightly heated in order to kill off any bacteria. Place room temperature eggs in a pan of cool water and bring the temperature of the water up to 140 °F for three minutes for large eggs. Immediately run the eggs under cool water and refrigerate them.

- Soft-boiled egg yolks are great in sauces and give them a satisfying thickness. To soft boil, add room temperatures eggs to a large pot of gently boiling water for 5 minutes, and then immediately remove the eggs and cool them under cool running water.

- Hard-boiled yolks are also fine to use in sauces, but since the yolks are dry and crumbly, they require a little altering in order to keep your sauce smooth and creamy. Extra mayo comes to mind. To hard boil eggs, follow the instructions for soft boiling, above, but leave the eggs in the water for 8 to 10 minutes.

FRESH GREEN SALSA

I was taught how to make this beautiful salsa by the distinguished Doña Rosa in Tepoztlan, Mexico, although no matter how I make it, I always do it wrong, according to her. This is a sign that you are in the presence of a great teacher. Green salsas are usually secondary to the red ones served in Mexican restaurants, but in the presence of good meat, it's the other way around.

> MAKES 1 CUP

4 to 6 green tomatillos, peeled of their papery skin.

1 small, white onion

2 cloves garlic

1 green jalapeño pepper and or 1 serrano pepper (optional for spice), remove stems and seeds.

⅓ cup chopped cilantro

1 teaspoon kosher salt

1. Bring a few cups of water to a boil in a large pot.

2. Quarter the tomatillos, and roughly chop the onion, and garlic.

3. Toss the vegetables and the pepper(s) in the water and boil them for 8 minutes.

4. Strain the tomatillos, onion, garlic, and pepper(s) and move them to a blender. Add about ⅓ cup of water (more or less) and do a quick blend. You want a chunky mixture, not a puree.

5. Finely chop the cilantro and put all ingredients into a nice serving bowl.

6. Add salt as desired.

7. The salsa will keep for at least a week in the refrigerator.

HEIRLOOM PICO DE GALLO

The only thing better than a good pico de gallo on your steak or chicken is a superb pico de gallo made from the finest ingredients. To really show off what this sauce can do, I add huge chunks of meaty, sweet, heirloom tomatoes.

> MAKES 1 CUP

1 small red onion

2 cipollini onions

1 bunch cilantro

1 basil leaf

3 or 4 tablespoons fresh lime juice

1 tablespoon olive oil

1 tablespoon fleur de sel

1 large, dense, heirloom tomato

1. With a razor-sharp knife, finely dice the onions, cilantro, and basil until the mixture resembles a thick pesto.

2. Add the lime juice and olive oil to the onion, cilantro, and basil mixture, and mix in the salt.

3. Slice or chop the tomato into the desired size and mix with the salsa.

4. Keep any leftover sauce in the refrigerator for a week or so in a covered jar.

HONEY JALAPEÑO SAUCE

I grew up being told that if I burned myself, I should "put some honey on it." When cooking with peppers, honey brings a sweet and soothing balance to the dish.

> MAKES: ½ CUP

4 tablespoons butter

4 teaspoons finely chopped jalapeño

4 tablespoons honey

1 tablespoon vinegar

4 tablespoons lime juice

1. In a small saucepan, add the butter and jalapeños and cook on low heat for 5 minutes.

2. Add honey, vinegar, and lime juice.

3. Stir the mixture well until it thickens. Remove from heat and let it cool.

HONEY MUSTARD BARBECUE SAUCE

This is a spin off the Basic Barbecue Sauce recipe on page 150 except the recipe uses pickle juice instead of straight vinegar and includes a dollop of mustard. It's a bit less sweet than the other barbecue recipe, and the mustard component lends it really well to hot dogs and sausages.

MAKES 1 CUP

1/2 medium white onion, diced

2 tablespoons olive oil

1 medium-large tomato

2 cloves garlic

1 1/2 tablespoons pickle juice

1 1/2 tablespoons yellow mustard

3 teaspoons honey

1 1/2 teaspoons soy sauce

3/4 teaspoon ground cayenne

3/4 teaspoon ground black or white pepper

1. In a small saucepan, caramelize the onion in the olive oil over low heat.

2. In a blender, puree the tomato and garlic.

3. In a separate saucepan, add the tomato and garlic puree and reduce it by one quarter over low heat.

4. Mix the caramelized onions with the tomato and garlic puree.

5. Mix in pickle juice, mustard, honey, and soy sauce.

6. Taste the sauce. It should be creamy and smooth. Slowly mix in the cayenne and black or white pepper. The cayenne will add spice and the pepper will add intensity, so add them slowly, tasting the sauce often, and find the right balance for you.

LECHE DE TIGRE SAUCE

This spicy, lime-based sauce is used for cooking with acid. It adds a nice zing to fish dishes. I particularly like to use it on dishes made with trout or scallops (see Scallops with *Leche de Tigre*, page 126).

MAKES 1 CUP

½ cup fresh lime juice

¼ cup orange juice

¼ habanero pepper, finely diced

3 cloves garlic, finely grated

¼ teaspoon grated ginger

3 tablespoons finely diced red onion

3 tablespoons freshly chopped cilantro

½ teaspoon kosher salt

Pinch of black pepper

1. Thoroughly mix the lime juice, orange juice, habanero pepper, garlic, ginger, onion, cilantro, salt, and pepper. Store in a sealed glass jar until ready for use.

LEMONATO SAUCE

Lemonato provides a solid foundation for, like, a million sauces, but I find that it's best on fish and salads. It's also quite tame. But, within moderation, a little serrano chile pepper adds crispness and bite.

MAKES 1 CUP

½ cup fresh lemon juice

½ cup olive oil

1 small serrano chile pepper, finely diced razor thin

Salt and pepper to taste

1. Thoroughly mix the lemon juice, olive oil, serrano chiles, salt, and pepper. Store the mixture in a resealable jar in the refrigerator for up to one week.

MEXICAN BULGOGI MARINADE

This marinade has made an appearance at almost every barbecue and pop-up I have done in the past 15 years. I use it on chicken drumsticks almost exclusively and have never received more compliments for any single dish. This marinade uses the main components of the distinguished recipe for classic Korean bulgogi marinade, but swaps out black pepper for some smoky chipotle (either the peppers or adobo sauce from a can of chipotle peppers).

> MAKES 2 CUPS

½ cups soy sauce

3 tablespoons adobo sauce from a can of chipotle

2 teaspoons ginger, minced

5 tablespoons white sugar

4 garlic cloves, minced

1 scallion, finely chopped (optional)

1. Mix together the soy sauce, adobo sauce, ginger, sugar, garlic, and scallions. Refrigerate the mixture for 4 to 24 hours to allow the flavors to blend.

THE SUGARS IN THE MEXICAN BULGOGI MARINADE WILL BURN VERY FAST OVER DIRECT HEAT, SO IF YOU ARE GRILLING FOODS THAT HAVE BEEN MARINATED IN THIS SAUCE, MAKE SURE TO COOK THEM OVER INDIRECT HEAT. TO USE THE MARINADE AS A SAUCE, PUT IT IN A PAN OVER MEDIUM-LOW HEAT AND REDUCE IT BY HALF.

MOLASSES BRINE

This brine adds dark coloring, sweetness, and some tanginess to cuts like pork chops or a chicken breast with ease and satisfaction.

MAKES 4 CUPS BRINE

4 cups water

¾ cup sugar

½ cup molasses

¼ cup salt

¼ cup sriracha

1. In a small saucepan, bring the water to a gentle boil.

2. Add sugar, molasses, salt, and sriracha.

3. Stir well and reduce heat to low. Let reduce by one-quarter. Remove from heat and refrigerate. This will keep in the refrigerator for up to 2 weeks (probably forever).

MOLASSES SAUCE

This sauce is a great accompaniment to most meats that gives touch of sweetness. When used as a glaze, it enables the crust to caramelize. I like to use it with Pork Tenderloin (page 87).

MAKES ⅓ CUPS

¼ cup soy sauce

¼ cup molasses

¼ cup white wine

1. Mix the soy sauce, molasses, and white wine in a small saucepan, and bring the mixture to a simmer.

2. Reduce the mixture by half. Remove from the heat and store in the refrigerator in a sealed glass jar until ready to use. The sauce can keep in the refrigerator for up to 2 weeks.

QUICK AIOLI

Distinguished guest: "Wow, this aioli is to die for! It's subtle, yet sophisticated. Me: "Thank you kindly! It is Hellman's, French's, and salt." This concoction makes cheap and lazy look good. If you're not feeling lazy, though, you can replace the olive oil with saffron olive oil.

▶ MAKES ½ CUP

½ cup mayonnaise

1 tablespoon olive oil or saffron-infused oil (see "Saffron Oil," page 165)

2 teaspoons classic yellow mustard

Handsome pinch of salt

1. Mix all the ingredients together in a small bowl, serve, and wait to hear all the "wows" from your guests.

2. This stuff will keep in the refrigerator for a few days, if there's any left over. Just keep it covered.

QUICK PICKLING BRINE

Pickling goes far back to a time when we don't even really know what folks did. The basics, as I know them, go into this recipe for a quick pickling option that can affect foods within an hour, become ideal in a day, and continue to add character over the next week or two.

▶ MAKES 6 CUPS

4 cups cold water

2 cups apple cider vinegar

⅓ cup white sugar (preferably ground to a powder; do not use confectioners' sugar)

3 tablespoons kosher salt

2 to 4 bay leaves

4 allspice berries, smashed

10 to 20 coriander seeds (whole)

1 teaspoon chopped dill

1. Combine the water, vinegar, sugar, kosher salt, bay leaves, allspice, berries, coriander seeds, and dill. Stir the ingredients well to dissolve the salt completely. (The sugar should dissolve easily as you mix the solution.) Set aside.

SAFFRON AIOLI

Steeping saffron in oil and using it for various applications can amplify its power. Using this oil in aioli creates a flavor profile that is deep but easy to like.

MAKES 1 CUP

1 tablespoon Saffron Oil (see below)

¾ cup mayonnaise

2 tablespoons classic yellow mustard

2 teaspoons kosher salt

1. Prepare the Saffron Oil at least 24 hours before you need to use it.

2. When the Saffron Oil is ready, mix the oil, mayonnaise, mustard, and salt together in a small bowl or jar. Keep it refrigerated until ready for use.

SAFFRON OIL

Saffron is the world's most expensive spice, not the least because it is harvested from a flower—the saffron crocus—and it takes about a quarter-million handpicked stigmata (also called threads) from the flowers to produce about one pound of saffron. However, you can steep a mere ¼ teaspoon of saffron in about ⅓ cup of olive oil and it will go a long way. After a week or so of steeping, it becomes quite a potent little mixture. Saffron oil is a great way to add dimension to Quick Aioli.

SIMPLE GLAZE

This glaze hits all the high notes, with Coca-Cola®, butter, and whiskey, respectively, as well as a dabble of gravy master to tie it all together. I also add a touch of fresh ginger as a salute to good health. It makes a great glaze for Caramelized Lamb Chops (page 79).

> MAKES ABOUT ¼ CUP

3 tablespoons Coca-Cola

½ teaspoon grated ginger

1½ tablespoons unsalted butter

½ teaspoon browning and seasoning sauce (e.g., Gravy Master®)

1 pinch kosher salt

1 teaspoon whiskey

1. In a pan, gently reduce Coca-Cola by one-third (about 5 to 10 minutes).

2. Add in ginger and stir briskly to incorporate.

3. Mix in the butter, browning and seasoning sauce, and salt.

4. Quickly whisk in the whiskey, remove the mixture from the heat, and brush the glaze over the meat right before serving or while the meat is still on the grill.

SWEET TARE GLAZE

Not only does this make a sweet glaze to cover chicken, it also can be used as a dip, to give extra sweetness to the dish! This makes a particularly tasty accompaniment to Candied Chicken Pops (page 98).

> MAKES 1 CUP

½ cup white wine

½ cup soy sauce

½ cup brown sugar

2 tablespoons thinly sliced ginger

1 tablespoon white vinegar

1. In a small saucepan, mix together the wine, soy sauce, brown sugar, ginger, and white vinegar. Heat the mixture over medium-low heat until it is reduced by one-quarter.

2. Remove the mixture from the heat. Take out the ginger from the glaze before serving.

TOYOMANSI

This versatile sauce is a classic in the Philippines, and variants of it can be found all over Southeast Asia. It's easy to make, is light, and can be used as a marinade for seafood, pork, and chicken wings. Toyomansi is so amenable that it can also serve as a dipping sauce and even salad dressing.

1. Thoroughly mix the soy sauce, clementine juice, garlic, scallion, and black pepper. (Add red pepper flakes as well, if you'd like.) Store in a sealed glass jar until ready to use.

> **MAKES ½ CUP**

¼ cup soy sauce

¼ cup fresh squeezed juice from 1 or 2 clementines

3 cloves garlic, grated or finely chopped

1 tablespoon scallion, thinly sliced

¼ teaspoon black pepper

Red pepper flakes (optional)

UMAMI BRINE

Phillip Gilmore is the owner of the restaurants Momos Sushi Shack, Moku Moku, and Hi Hello in Bushwick, Brooklyn. He was head bartender at Sweet Ups, runs Heritage Radio Network, is friends with literally everyone in the food scene in Brooklyn, and is a dear friend of mine. His riffs and takes on Japanese cuisine know no bounds, and I have learned a great deal from what he has served me at his restaurants. This recipe is inspired by Momo's decadent umami pork dish.

MAKES 6 CUPS OF BRINE

6 cups water

1 tablespoon salt

½ cup light brown sugar

5 to 6 shitake mushrooms (preferably dried)

1 cup dried seaweed

1 teaspoon blue cheese

1. In a saucepan, mix together the water, salt, and sugar.

2. Bring the mixture to a simmer to fully dissolve the salt and sugar. Then add the mushrooms, seaweed, and blue cheese. Stir well, and let the brine cool.

3. When the brine is cool, put it in a glass, sealable container. Keep it refrigerated. The brine can keep for up to 1 week.

WHISKEY SAUCE

This sauce is sweet and boozy and is a big hit at parties. I serve it up with chicken wings, burgers, and steaks. It's pretty intense and, depending on how much booze you want to use, it can distract your taste buds from the more delicate flavors in the sauce.

MAKES ABOUT ½ CUP

4 tablespoons butter

Pinch salt

2 tablespoons light brown sugar

2 tablespoons maple syrup

2 tablespoons apple cider vinegar

1 shot (2 ounces) whiskey (plus a shot to drink just to make sure the whiskey is good)

1. Melt the butter in a pan over low heat. Cook the mixture until the butter turns brown.

2. Add the light brown sugar and maple syrup, and cook over low heat, while stirring. Once the sauce begins to get thick, burnt, and sticky, add the vinegar. Stir the mixture gently for 1 minute.

3. Pour 1 to 2 ounces of whiskey into mixture. You can cook off the alcohol or not.

4. Add salt to taste.

5. Add more vinegar or whiskey to loosen the mixture as desired.

9

SIDE DISHES

When my wife, Gladys, first introduced me to my now in-laws, we had a Cameroonian dinner. There was a big table in the corner of the room adorned with large, foil baking trays, each piled high with a mix of traditional dishes: *Ndole*, a dish that uses bitter leaves similar to spinach, oxtail, shrimp, and nuts; *Bobolo*, steamed yucca rolled in banana leaves; beignet balls (doughnuts for dinner!); and perhaps another six trays containing variations and combinations of beans, chicken, and fish.

This extravagant buffet had no central theme but was a collection of flavors and textures that could be combined according to whim. Oftentimes supporting characters can steal the show. The ones in this chapter are made with familiarity and comfort in mind.

BEIGNETS

Instead of plain-old store-bought hamburger buns, why not try a beignet? They add a nice touch of added flavor to grilled meat. This beignet recipe doesn't even use yeast, takes 2 minutes to prep, and, by simply adding more sugar or fruit, can be made into sweet doughnuts for dessert. It's a win-win—and the perfect antidote to baking anxiety. These Beignets are particularly good with the Beignet Classic Burger (page 30).

MAKES ABOUT 10 BUNS

5 cups all-purpose flour (plus a little extra for your hands)

8 teaspoons brown sugar

4 teaspoons baking powder

1 teaspoon kosher salt

4 cups buttermilk

Peanut oil for frying, about ½ gallon

1. Combine all dry ingredients, making sure to break up any chunks of brown sugar.

2. Gently incorporate the buttermilk. Be careful to mix just enough so there are no pockets of dry powder. You do not want to overwork the dough or the beignets will be tough.

3. Flour your hands and pinch off a piece of dough the size of a raquet ball.

4. Making sure not to overwork the dough, shape the dough into a disc shape, about ¾ inch thick. (They do not have to be a perfect shape!)

5. Fill a large saucepan with the peanut oil. If you have a tabletop deep fryer, use the recommended amount. If you don't, you'll need about ½ gallon. Heat it until it reaches 375 degrees. Drop the beignets into the hot oil for 6 to 8 minutes.

6. Remove the beignets from the oil and gently pat them dry with paper towels.

7. To avoid burning yourself, cradle a beignet in a dishcloth or paper towel. Then cut the bun and load it up.

CHILI

On a scale from 1 to 10, even terrible chili starts around 5. You have to try very hard to really screw it up. And yet, to achieve perfection is perhaps unattainable. Chili is at the epicenter of many cook-offs, it's found in all barbecue establishments, and it's often thrown on hot dogs. It's a cowboy food, born in the all-or-nothing days of the Wild West. It embraces all the foods of the Americas equally—beans, corn, chilies, tomatoes, and meats. There are no bounds to chili. One can interpret it endlessly. In fact, I have never cooked the same chili twice. But there are some guidelines to get a chili just right, mainly by building it in layers (see "Building a Great Chili," on page 175). Chili is a living organism, a layered system that evolves, matures, and in the end gets devoured with rapturous delight.

MAKES: 8 CUPS

FOR THE BASE

¼ cup butter or rendered fat (duck, bacon, smoked bacon, or butter)

½ large white onion, diced

¼ cup white flour

1 cup milk

1½ cups meat. I often use the leftovers from sausages, preferably Beef Rib & Marrow (page 54)

2 teaspoons kosher salt, to taste

2 teaspoons coarsely ground black pepper, to taste

FOR THE SECOND LAYER

3 cups precooked beans, rinsed

2 cups chopped tomato

1½ cups leek, thinly sliced

1 cup sweet corn kernels

3 tablespoons sugar, maple syrup, or honey (optional, to taste, depending on desired sweetness)

FOR THE THIRD LAYER

1 teaspoon paprika (optional)

2 tablespoons chipotle adobo sauce (optional)

1 tablespoon fresh herbs such as thyme

¼ cup finely chopped red onion

PREPARING THE BASE

1. In a large, deep pan or pot, add the fat and white onion.

2. Cook over medium-low heat, stirring the onion constantly, until it starts to brown (in about 15 minutes).

3. Whisk in the flour slowly and cook for an additional 3 minutes.

4. Slowly add the milk while whisking.

5. Stir in meat and cook for 5 more minutes.

6. Add a couple pinches of salt and pepper to taste.

PREPARING THE SECOND LAYER

1. Add the chopped tomatoes, leek, and corn. Cook the mixture for 10 minutes. If at any point, it becomes too thick, add some milk or water, $\frac{1}{3}$ of a cup at a time.

2. Add sugar, syrup, or honey to taste.

PREPARING THE THIRD LAYER

1. Add beans to the pot.

2. Mix in paprika and or chipotle, $\frac{1}{2}$ teaspoon at a time, to taste.

3. Add fresh herbs, $\frac{1}{2}$ teaspoon at a time, to taste.

4. Mix in raw red onion and more fresh ground black pepper, to taste. Serve.

BUILDING A GREAT CHILI

There are layers in chili on which to build. For me, there are at least three—each of which has a particular duty. Unless you want a bean salad, you're going to want a creamy base. This is the job of the first layer. I make a roux, and when I'm feeling particularly rambunctious, I use clarified duck fat instead of butter. For a heavy, meaty base, the roux can then take on ground or chopped meat.

The second layer is made up of beans, tomatoes and corn, and other cooked vegetables. Here, there's a great opportunity to make some aesthetic decisions about texture and color. How big do you want to cut the tomatoes? Which colored ones do you want to use? The same choices apply to beans and other veggies.

The third layer comes at the end, and is composed of uncooked vegetables and spices. Yes the spices can be added anywhere along the line, but at the end, you can already taste your chili and better understand in what direction you want it to go. Here is where the whole dish gets rounded out and you can provide balance. I love, for example, adding freshly chopped red onion right before serving—its bite and crunch, freshness and aroma really add brightness to chili and bring out some of its deeper flavors.

CRUNCHY AVOCADO CRACKERS

I don't know about you, but when I was growing up in New Hampshire, we did not grill avocados! I bet before the Internet came to town most people had no idea what the hell an avocado even was. Around there, back then, if it didn't take gasoline or 30/30 cartridges, it was a nonissue. Today avocados are having their moment of fame. It seems like every day I read about some hot new chef who's reinvented the avocado in some "rapturously sinful" way.

Avocados are cool, rich, creamy, and dense. Because of that texture, they slice easily. The problem is they get a bit delicate on the grill when sliced. But there is a solution! Apply a dry rub that forms a caramelized crust around each slice.

> **MAKES 4 OR 5 SNACKS**

Quick Aioli (page 164)

Eel Sauce (page 156)

2 ripe avocados

1 large egg

6 tablespoons panko flakes

1 tablespoon kosher salt

1 tablespoon small ancho chile flakes

1 tablespoon light brown sugar

EQUIPMENT

Pastry brush

1. Prepare quick the Quick Aioli and Eel Sauce in advance. Refrigerate until ready to use.

2. Bring the grill up to medium heat.

3. Cut each avocado in half, holding the side with the pit facing upward. Give it a good whack with a knife and twist to free the pit. Discard the seeds.

4. With the skin still on, slice each half of the avocado into 4 wedges.

5. In a bowl, beat the egg and paint it on the cut faces of the avocado wedges with a pastry brush.

6. Gently crumble the panko flakes and toast until bone dry.

7. In a small bowl, mix together the panko flakes, salt, chile flakes, and sugar. Place the dry mixure onto a small plate.

8. Gently peel each avocado slice. Lightly cover all sides of each avocado wedge with beaten egg and then the dry mixture.

9. Thoroughly clean and oil the grill.

10. Grill the slices or wedges for 3 to 4 minutes on each side until they are crispy.

11. Serve the avocado with Quick Aioli and Eel Sauce.

> THE PERFECT AVOCADO SHOULD BE FIRM WHEN PRESSED, BUT NOT HARD. IF IT'S EFFORTLESS TO MAKE THUMBPRINTS, IT'S TOO RIPE AND NO GOOD.

FIG COMPOTE

It's seldom I come across fresh black figs in the market, but when I do I scoop them up to make this recipe, the perfect complement to smoky pork dishes. Baby-back ribs come to mind, but it also pairs beautifully with all kinds of grilled chicken.

MAKES 1 CUP

10 black figs

2 to 3 tablespoons butter

2 tablespoons white wine (or beer)

¼ cup honey

¼ teaspoon herbes de Provence

½ teaspoon ground allspice

Salt and fresh ground pepper to taste

1. Cut the figs in half and add them to a small saucepan with the butter.

2. Cook the figs and butter over medium heat until they are soft, about 5 minutes.

3. Add the wine or beer to the fig mixture and cook it for another minute or so.

4. And the honey, herbes de Provence, and allspice to the mixture, blend it well, and cook it for another 2 to 3 minutes.

5. Serve the compote with a little salt and pepper to taste.

GRILLED BUTTERMILK BISCUITS

Arguably the greatest invention since beer, buttermilk biscuits make everyone happy, and they are also easy to make. The first month I started making biscuits, I gained 20 pounds. I was struggling and in denial. They are so cheap and so fast and easy to make that surely one more baker's dozen before work won't harm anyone! These biscuits can also be made on the grill next to your other fixings.

MAKES 6 TO 10 BISCUITS

2 cups all-purpose flour

1 tablespoon baking powder

$\frac{1}{2}$ teaspoon fine salt

1 stick cold, hard butter

1$\frac{1}{2}$ cups buttermilk (or use regular whole milk with a squirt of lemon juice or vinegar)

2 tablespoons honey (optional)

1. Bring the grill to medium-high heat.

2. In a mixing bowl, combine flour, baking powder, and salt. Set the mixture aside.

3. On a cutting board, use a large kitchen knife to cut the butter in half lengthwise. The butter must be cold for this recipe. Then cut each of the lengths in half, and cut each of the halves in half once more. Stack them together together and chop the butter into small cubes.

4. Scatter the cold butter cubes throughout the flour mixture and, incorporate them with a fork. I use two forks, one to press down on the cubes of butter and the other to scrape the butter from the fork. Continue cutting the butter into the flour until you have pea-sized crumbles.

5. Next, slowly fold in the buttermilk. You should be left with a wet, sticky mess.

6. Wet your hands with water, and then grab a jumbo-egg-sized glob of the dough. Form it into a small puck, and place it on a buttered pan or sheet. Repeat this process until you've used all of the dough.

7. Leave some room around each of the biscuits, as they will increase in size by about 50 percent.

8. Grill or bake the biscuits for 15 to 20 minutes, or until they are golden brown.

9. Serve the biscuits warm and, if you'd like, add a drizzle of honey.

GRILLED CORN ELOTE SALAD

Elote is a classic street food in Mexico, where grilled corn is slathered with mayonnaise and some dried, crumbly cheese like queso seco, and then of course hit with some chile. This tried-and-true combo also sets the tone for a great grilled salad.

SERVES 4

4 ears of corn

4 tablespoons mayonnaise

½ cup Parmesan cheese, shaved

1 cup endive, roughly chopped

1 cup baby arugula

10 cherry tomatoes, halved

1 tablespoon chile flakes

Salt and pepper to taste

1. Grill the corn in the husks over medium-low heat for 20 minutes, rotating them often.

2. Remove the husks and grill the cobs until they are lightly charred.

3. Remove the corn from the heat and allow it to cool.

4. With a knife, cut off the corn kernels and mix them with mayonnaise and cheese in a salad bowl.

5. Mix in the endive, arugula, and tomatoes.

6. Add the chile flakes. Anything can be used: pasilla, ancho, pasilla, etc. Each lend a unique perspective.

7. Add salt and pepper to taste.

GRILLED YUKON GOLD POTATOES WITH EGG YOLK AIOLI

I like all potatoes, but Yukon Golds are about as delicate and pretty as a potato can be. They also don't really need to be peeled, which makes them easy to make when you're already busy prepping and grilling lots of other things.

> MAKES 4 SMALL SIDES

½ cup Egg Yolk Aioli (page 157)

8 Yukon Gold potatoes

¼ cup olive oil

4 cloves garlic, crushed

1 tablespoon Maldon salt, divided use

EQUIPMENT

36-inch-long sheet of heavy-duty aluminum foil

1. Prepare the Egg Yolk Aioli in advance.

2. Bring the grill to medium heat.

3. Wash the potatoes and cut them in half through the widest part of the potato.

4. Rip off a 36-inch-long sheet of aluminum foil and fold it in half to measure 18 inches long. Lay the foil on a flat surface.

5. Spread half the oil over the foil with your hands, or apply it with a paper towel, and then sprinkle the foil with half the salt and all of the garlic.

6. Lay the potatoes face down and close together on one half of the foil. Cover the tops of the potatoes with the remaining oil and salt.

7. Fold the other half of the foil over the potatoes, and press the top layer of foil around the potatoes so that you can clearly see their outlines.

8. Crimp and seal the edges of the foil so that no oil escapes.

9. When the grill is ready, grill the potatoes with the flat, cut-side up for 15 minutes. Flip them over, and grill them cut-side down for another 15 minutes.

10. Remove the potatoes from the heat, and gently peel the foil away from cut side, revealing a crispy golden crust.

11. Let them cool. Mix with the Egg Yolk Aioli or serve it alongside the potatoes in a small bowl.

LEX'S PICKLES

When I was young(er), I remember digging through hamburgers to find the pickle, which I would promptly discard in disgust. Young kids don't like low-calorie and acidic foods (vegetables) in general, probably as an evolutionary thing, a throwback to a time when meat and carbs, loaded with fats and energy, were the producers of growth and strength. As we grow older, nutrient-packed fruits and vegetables become our friends. Pickling is an ancient art used to preserve food for travel and winter.

MAKES 6 CUPS

Quick Pickling Brine (page 164)
3 to 4 small cucumbers, sliced about ⅛-inch thick

1. Prepare the Quick Pickling Brine.

2. Place the sliced cucumbers in a large glass jar with a resealable lid, such as a glass canning jar.

2. Fill it to the top with the Quick Pickling Brine. Keep the jar sealed and refrigerated for at least 24 hours and up to 2 weeks.

PEAR JELLY

Pears make a great jelly because they are smooth and flavorful, and they are not boastful like other fruits. Like apples they are easy to enjoy, but they have a degree of class that sets them apart.

> **MAKES 1 CUP**

2 tablespoons unsalted butter

2 ripe green Anjou pears, peeled and thinly sliced

⅛ teaspoon herbes de Provence

⅛ teaspoon allspice

2 tablespoons honey

1. Add the butter and pears to a saucepan over medium heat and caramelize the pears (about 15 minutes).

2. Add in the herbs, allspice, and honey, and cook an additional 5 minutes on low heat.

3. Set the mixture aside to cool a bit before serving.

QUICK PICKLED VEGETABLES

Pickling your own vegetables is fast and easy, and you can't screw them up. Quick preparation simply entails marinating your choice of veggies (or fruits) for a few hours—just enough time to imbue them with the flavors in your brine while giving them sweetness and a crispy bite from the vinegar. You can pickle just about anything you have laying around the house.

MAKES 1 TO 2 CUPS

3 cups Quick Pickling Brine (page 164)

4 jalapeños

2 colorful, heirloom carrots, skinned and cut lengthwise

½ small, red onion sliced pole to pole ¼-inch thick

1. Prepare the Pickling Brine.

2. Place all the vegetables in a large glass jar with a resealable lid, such as a glass canning jar.

3. Fill it to the top with the Pickling Brine. Keep the jar sealed and refrigerated for at least 24 hours and up to 2 weeks.

RUSTIC BREAD

I am sympathetic to folks who forgo making their own buns and settle for store-bought rolls. After all, cooking over flames and smoke is already an honorable task. But, if you truly want a great grilling experience, nothing beats pairing delicious meats and sauces with fresh, warm, pillow-soft bread and buns with a crispy, golden outer shell.

MAKES: 2 LOAVES OR 16 BUNS

2 cups warm water

1 tablespoon white sugar

1 tablespoon yeast (make sure it's fresh)

4 cups bread flour

4 tablespoons butter

2 tablespoons honey

1 to 2 teaspoons Maldon salt

Basting brush

1. Measure 2 cups of water in a saucepan and heat it until it is warm to the touch.

2. Mix in the sugar and yeast, and let the mixture sit for 5 to 10 minutes until it becomes frothy.

3. In a mixing bowl, add 3 cups of the bread flour and mix in the water. This should result in a very wet and sticky mess. Slowly add in the last cup of flour while mixing the dough by hand.

4. Once the dough turns into a soft and manageable ball, kneed it on a floured surface. The dough should remain sticky. Kneed the dough for 2 to 3 minutes more.

5. Transfer the dough to an oiled bowl and cover it with a clean dishtowel. Let the dough rest until it has doubled in size, from 30 to 60 minutes.

6. Remove the dough from the bowl and transfer it to a lightly floured surface. Gently punch down the ball of dough and shape it back into a ball. Do not overwork the dough.

7. Cut the ball of dough into 16 equal-sized pieces. To make hamburger buns, form the dough into thin pucks, about 1 inch high. To make hotdog buns, press the dough into rectangular pieces, about 1/2 inch thick and roughly the size of a postcard.

8. Let the dough rest for 5 minutes while you prepare the glaze. Over low heat, melt the butter and stir in the honey and salt.

9. With a basting brush generously paint the buns on all sides. To shape the hot dog buns, fold the dough in half lengthwise after basting. This will make it easy to pry open the buns after cooking. You can cut the hamburger buns in half with a knife.

10. Grill the buns over indirect HIGH heat—500 to 550 degrees for 8 to 10 minutes. Serve right away.

SESAME-CUCUMBER SALAD

This is a simple salad that is both cool and refreshing on the palate. It compliments fatty steaks and burgers well and is a breeze to make.

SERVES 2 TO 4 PEOPLE

1 seedless cucumber

1 tablespoon sesame oil

1 teaspoon black sesame seeds

1 teaspoon salt.

1. Cut cucumber into small wedges or $\frac{1}{2}$-inch cubes.

2. In a salad bowl, mix the cucumber, sesame oil, and sesame seeds. Chill the mixture and add the salt just before serving.

SPICY GRILLED PINEAPPLE KEBABS

Grilled pineapple is a sweet, hot, juicy mess that cuts through the fat and grease on all the sizzling meats we grill. Thin pineapple slices also make a great bed on the grill to protect delicate fish. But for a slightly less messy snack, smaller pieces on kebabs are quick and easy to grill.

MAKES SNACKS FOR 4

$\frac{1}{2}$ pineapple, peeled, and cut into 1-inch cubes

$\frac{1}{2}$ teaspoon ground cumin

$\frac{1}{4}$ teaspoon rosemary

Salt to taste

Equipment

4 metal skewers or water-soaked wood skewers

1. Bring the grill to medium heat.

2. Place 6 to 8 pineapple cubes on a metal kebab or on a thoroughly damp wood skewer.

3. Mix all of the dry ingredients in a small bowl and sprinkle the mix over the pineapple.

4. Grill the pineapple kebabs for 2 minutes per side for a total of 8 minutes.

10

A DRINK OR TWO

The Bar de Los Amigos is located at the end of a muddy alley in the cloud-forest town of Santa Elena, Costa Rica. It's a real dump by all accounts. The entrance is completely blocked by dirt bikes in all levels of disrepair. Inside it is dark and wet and smells like a Lower East Side dive, complete with humidity, dirt, and bugs.

The seating is all plastic and promotional-looking. Some seats are cracked; others, with missing legs, have been thrown into a corner. The light over the pool table is frustratingly misplaced, and there are rolls of chicken wire and damp Imperial beer boxes.

No women are here, no bumbling tourists—just "los amigos." And within an hour of arriving, I've met more locals than I did during the first two weeks I was in town. We spend hours drinking and smoking, and by the end of it all, I've been invited to just about everyone's house.

Behind the bar there's a barely noticeable hole with a curtain over it. Every now and then a tiny hand slides out a plate holding a small tortilla with a cube of meat and some gravy. What a treat! Oftentimes in a place like this the food may raise eyebrows, but among great people and flowing beers, these dainty morsels slide quietly off the "do not eat" list.

Back home, when grilling with friends and family, I love to pair good food and company with good drink. Though I am not a bartender, the following drinks always make a big impression on my guests and can provide exuberance and a good balance to any meal.

BLACKBERRY BOURBON

For a fat-free whiskey drink, try steeping some fresh blackberries in your favorite (or least favorite) bourbon. Blackberries have a simple but elegant flavor, stay firm in liquid, and have a nice little crunch to boot. Garnish the drink with a little lime to add a bit of color and clarity.

> **MAKES 1 BOTTLE OF BOURBON**

750 milliliters bourbon like High West® or Bulleit™

1 cup blackberries

5 mint leaves or to taste, chopped

3 to 5 allspice berries

5 to 10 whole black peppercorns

EQUIPMENT

1 large glass jar with a tightly sealing lid

1. Pour 1 cup of the bourbon into a lidded jar.

2. Wash the blackberries and gently break them up.

3. Add the blackberries, chopped mint leaves, and the allspice and the pepper to the bottle.

4. Shake the bottle or stir the contents, and let the bottle sit for at least a day before serving.

HORSERADISH VODKA

Jarring up fruits and herbs with your vodka is a great way to impart flavor while keeping it stiff. With a quality vodka, such as Grey Goose, and served chilled, this can make for smooth, intoxicating bliss. Horseradish-infused vodka is strong and classy, and if you're up for a mixed drink, it can serve as a solid base.

MAKES 1 BOTTLE OF VODKA

750 milliliters vodka

1 fresh horseradish root, about 5 inches long, peeled and cut

EQUIPMENT

1 large glass jar with a tight-fitting lid

1. Pour the entire bottle of vodka into a resealable glass jar. Store in a cool place.

2. Fresh horseradish is very potent and will impart a strong flavor to the vodka in a matter of hours. If you plan on storing the vodka for a while, a smaller chunk of horseradish will do. If you want to serve the vodka the same day, cut the horseradish into smaller pieces so there's more surface area exposed to the vodka.

3. Add the desired amount of horseradish to the vodka, seal the jar, and store it until ready for use.

MICHELADA

Mexican beers are among my favorites, maybe because of the climate, the beach… the drinkability. They're just great. The Michelada takes beer to the next level by adding an assortment of ingredients— lime juice, chiles, tomato juice, etc. You can customize the ingredients in a Michelada to pair excitingly and appropriately with any meal. You can also try this recipe with any beer you want, but I highly suggest using an easy swilling brew that's not flavored with pumpkins. Seriously, who drinks that crap anyway?

MAKES 6 DRINKS, 12 OUNCES EACH

1 cup tomato juice or tomato-vegetable juice

1 tablespoon chili flakes

¼ teaspoon beef bouillon granules

2 limes, halved

2 tablespoons coarse sea salt

6 cans of your favorite, non-pumpkin-flavored, beer

1 lime, cut in 6 wedges for serving

1. Mix the tomato juice or tomato-vegetable juice, chili flakes, and bullion in a jar.

2. Cut the limes in half and squeeze them into the tomato mix. Reserve the halves to use in step 4.

3. Sprinkle the salt onto a small plate.

4. Cut the used lime halves into wedges, and rub the rims of the glasses to moisten them. Then dip the glass rims into the salt.

5. Pour each beer into a prepared glass, and add some ice cubes, leaving enough room for an ounce of tomato juice.

6. Pour 1 ounce of the tomato juice into the beer, stir, and serve with a wedge of lime.

MANGORITA

When I dream of paradise it's a day spent snorkeling in Akumal Bay, Mexico, followed by some deep-sea fishing, a nap, and then, at night, grilling the day's catch and sipping on Mangoritas. They're strong and intense, like a margarita, but with a smoother and creamier finish.

> **MAKES 4 SERVINGS, 6 OUNCES EACH**

2 tablespoons coarse sea salt

2 ounces fresh squeezed lime juice (reserving the used lime halves)

8 ounces tequila

4 ounces triple sec

10 ounces mango nectar

1. In a small bowl, mix the spices together.

2. Place the salt in a small, flat dish big enough to fit the rim of a glass.

3. Using the reserved lime halves, cut a wedge of lime and run it around the rims of the glasses to wet them.

4. Dip the rims of the glasses in the salt and spice mixtures to coat them thoroughly.

5. Pour the tequila, triple sec, lime juice, and mango nectar into a pitcher and stir.

6. Pour the drinks over ice into the prepared glasses and serve.

PICKLE BACK CHASER

I was a regular at the Bushwick Country Club in Brooklyn, when this drink made its debut there. It was definitely a revelation. Pickles and grilling go hand in hand, and if you're a responsible grill master, you'll always be sure to have some pickle juice lying around. If not, it's never too late to start pickling!

> **MAKES 4 CHASER SHOTS**

4 ounces dill pickle juice (brand of your choice)

1. Strain the pickle juice to remove any seeds or spices.

2. Pour into a 1-ounce shot glass to chase your favorite whiskey.

SMOKED PIG WHISKEY

We're not reinventing the wheel here; we're just greasing the axle. Reduced fats from the grill can be collected and used to enlighten even the most godless whiskeys. When grilling with a wood-smoke fire, I'll usually put some of my fat trimmings in a small cast iron pan in a corner of the grill to let it smoke. I've tried this process with bacon, jowl, lardo, pancetta, pork chop fat, duck fat, and beef bone marrow. I find the best outcomes come from natural, smoked bacon and cured jowl.

This Smoked Pig Whiskey needs to be prepared at least 24 hours in advance of when you intend to serve it.

MAKES 1 BOTTLE OF WHISKEY

1 cup pork fat

750 milliliters inexpensive bourbon, such as Old Crow® or Evan Williams® or Jim Beam®

EQUIPMENT

1 large glass jar with a tight-fitting lid

1 large pouring pitcher or other large jar

3 coffee filters

1 funnel

1. Tenderly cut the fat into small slivers and cook them in a pan over low heat.

2. Cook the fat slowly so that it renders as a clear liquid. Pour out the clear liquid into a heat-proof bowl.

3. Pour the whiskey into a large, sealable glass jar. (If you add the fat directly to the whiskey bottle you may have a hard time getting it out and you will have to transfer the whiskey to a decanter.)

4. Using a funnel, pour the fat into the whiskey and stir vigorously.

5. Pour the whiskey into the glass jar. Be sure to seal the top securely, because alcohol evaporates very quickly and we are not shooting for fat-washed water here.

6. Let the whiskey sit overnight at room temperature, though you may get decent results in a matter of hours, depending on the intensity of the fat flavor.

7. Place the jar of whiskey into the freezer for 2 hours. The whiskey will not freeze, but the fats will rise and coagulate at the top of the jar.

8. Place a coffee filter inside the funnel, and pour the whiskey back into its bottle or into a decanter, depending on what you did in step 3. This will collect all the frozen fat globules.

9. Taste the whiskey. It should not be greasy. If it is, repeat step 7 and 8.

10. Serve the whiskey straight or mix it as you normally would.

METRIC CONVERSION CHARTS

The recipes that appear in this cookbook use the standard United States method for measuring liquid and dry or solid ingredients (teaspoons, tablespoons, and cups). The information on this chart is provided to help cooks outside the U.S. successfully use these recipes. All equivalents are approximate.

METRIC EQUIVALENTS FOR DIFFERENT TYPES OF INGREDIENTS

STANDARD CUP	FINE POWDER (e.g. flour)	GRAIN (e.g. rice)	GRANULAR (e.g. sugar)	LIQUID SOLIDS (e.g. butter)	LIQUID (e.g. milk)
3/4	105 g	113 g	143 g	150 g	180 ml
2/3	93 g	100 g	125 g	133 g	160 ml
1/2	70 g	75 g	95 g	100 g	120 ml
1/3	47 g	50 g	63 g	67 g	80 ml
1/4	35 g	38 g	48 g	50 g	60 ml
1/8	18 g	19 g	24 g	25 g	30 ml

USEFUL EQUIVALENTS FOR LIQUID INGREDIENTS BY VOLUME

1/4 tsp		=					1 ml	
1/2 tsp		=					2 ml	
1 tsp	=						5 ml	
3 tsp	=	1 tbls	=		1/2 fl oz	=	15 ml	
		2 tbls	=	1/8 cup	=	1 fl oz	=	30 ml
		4 tbls	=	1/4 cup	=	2 fl oz	=	60 ml
		5 1/8 tbls	=	1/3 cup	=	3 fl oz	=	80 ml
		8 tbls	=	1/2 cup	=	4 fl oz	=	120 ml
		10 2/8 tbls	=	2/3 cup	=	5 fl oz	=	160 ml
		12 tbls	=	3/4 cup	=	6 fl oz	=	180 ml
		16 tbls	=	1 cup	=	8 fl oz	=	240 ml
		1 pt	=	2 cups	=	16 fl oz	=	480 ml
		1 qt	=	4 cups	=	32 fl oz	=	960 ml
						33 fl oz	=	1000 ml= 1 L

USEFUL EQUIVALENTS FOR DRY INGREDIENTS BY WEIGHT

(To convert ounces to grams, multiply the number of ounces by 30.)

1 oz	=	1/16 lb	=	28.3 g	
4 oz	=	1/4 lb	=	113 g	
8 oz	=	1/2 lb	=	227 g	
12 oz	=	3/4 lb	=	340 g	
16 oz	=	1 lb	=	454 g	

ACKNOWLEDGMENTS

Dear Mom, you instilled in me the mantra that hard work and focus would save me from a life of "flipping burgers." Being dyslexic, I understood it to mean that flipping burgers would save me from a life of "work." Anyway, I thank you for direction and purpose.

Thank you Dad—you had me believe for years that you invented Toad in the Hole (you called it Moon over Miami), and that I too could invent something as lofty as burnt toast with a hole poked out and an egg inside. This has taught me to aim high.

I'd like to thank my children, Mateo and Zoe, for your youthful enthusiasm, exhaustive judgment, and critical palates regarding our family dinners. You have taught me the virtues of patience, meditation, and butter.

Thank you, my dear wife, Gladys, who reminds me daily that it's not okay to incessantly cook pork belly. You have taught me how to compromise.

Dear Victor, my good friend, who eats without shame or modesty (or utensils). You taught me how to recklessly enjoy food. Thank you very much.

Thank you, Frankie, for being supportive and nurturing, even when I've lost my mind.

Thank you, Grandma, for never telling me what's in your cooking! Mystery and curiosity are the cornerstones of creativity.

Thank you, dear Kenya, for opening my eyes to the beauty of what we eat.

And to Phil, who showed me that no matter what or how people eat, they always love a good show.

PHOTO CREDITS

INDEX

Burgers (cont.)

Beignet Classic Burger, 30–31

Bourgeois Burger, 38

Burger with Fig Compote, 36–37

Cheese-Stuffed Meatball Sliders
with Whiskey Sauce, 29

Classic Burger, 27–28

Mushroom Burger, 32–33

Shrimp Burger, 34

Swedish Meatball Burger, 35

Butter, browned with tarragon, 151

Buttermilk biscuits, grilled, 179

Buttermilk Marinade, 152

C

Calzone, grilled chicken, 110

Cameroon, Douala in, 134–135

Campfire, grilling over, 13–15

Canadian arctic, seafood and,
113–115

Candied Chicken Pops, 98–100

Cans, for cooking, 19

Caramelized Lamb Chops, 78–79

Carrots, pickled, 186–187

Cast iron pans, 18

Chain, leg of lamb on, 76–77

Char, herb-blazed arctic, 116–117

Charcoal

adding to fire, 5, 11–12

briquettes, 5, 9

chimney, 2, 3, 5, 17

comparison of types, 9

"instant light" briquettes, 5

lump, 5, 9

starting fire, 2, 3

Cheese

Beignet Classic Burger, 30–31

Cheese-Stuffed Meatball Sliders
with Whiskey Sauce, 29

Mushroom Burger, 32–33

Chicken. See Poultry

Chile de Arbol Salsa, 153

Chiles, for sauces, 93. See also Rubs
and salts; Sauces, salsas, and
marinades

Chili, 174–175

Chimichurri Hot Dog, 43

Chimichurri Sauce, 154

Chimney, charcoal, 2, 3, 5, 17

Citrus

Leche de Tigre Sauce, 161

Lemonato Sauce, 161

Clams, grilled littleneck, 124–125

Classic Burger, 27–28

Cleaning grills, 12

Cleavers, 16

Coconut Curry Sauce, 155

Corn

Chiles, for sauces, 174–175

Grilled Corn Elote Salad,
180–181

Cornish hen, stuffed on a stake,
106–107

Crunchy Avocado Crackers, 176–177

Crunchy Black Branzino with
Lemonato Sauce, 120–121

Cucumbers

Cucumber Aioli, 155

Sesame-Cucumber Salad, 191

D

Dark Rub, 138

Denaturation, 83

Direct grilling, 2–4

Douala, Cameroon, 134–135

Double-Baked Chicken Thighs, 101

Drinks

about: Bar de Los Amigos in Costa
Rica and, 193

Blackberry Bourbon, 194–195

Horseradish Vodka, 196

Mangorita, 199

Michelada, 197

Pickle Back Chaser, 199

Smoked Pig Whiskey, 200–201

Duck, whole with honey and
cantaloupe, 108–109

Duck dogs, sweet, 46

E

Eel Sauce, 156

Eggs

about: using in sauces, 157

Egg Yolk Aioli, 157

Grilled Yukon Gold Potatoes with
Egg Yolk Aioli, 182

F

Fats (trimmed), using, 65

Figs

Burger with Fig Compote, 36–37

Fig Compote, 178

Ribs and Figs, 84–85

Fire

for briquettes or lump coal, 2

campfires, rotisserie and, 13–15

ABOUT THE AUTHOR

Lex Taylor is a chef, traveler, and master of grilling, barbecue, and smoking. Lex runs pop-ups in New York City at restaurants, bars, and special events, and for 15 years he has been serving up classic American barbecue and epic grilled meats, inspired by techniques he learned while traveling in the Americas, the Caribbean, Africa, Asia, and the Middle East. He uses skills acquired from cooking just about everywhere, from Mexican fishing enclaves to the floe edge of Inuit hunting camps. Lex's interests also include pickling, sausage making, knife making, leather craft, and the outdoors. Lex recently won Esquire TV's *The Next Great Burger* contest with his New Orleans inspired Classic Beignet Burger, a deep-fried burger with saffron aioli and sweet heirloom tomatoes served on a beignet.